TAKING HOSPICE TO THE MOUNTAINS

A NURSE'S STORY

by

CAROLYN PINION RICE

ISBN: 1468077937
ISBN 13: 9781468077933

"… I know the plans I have for you," says the Lord.
"They are plans for good…."

Jeremiah 29:11

*Dedicated to the staff and volunteers of
Prospect Home Care and Hospice*

CONTENTS

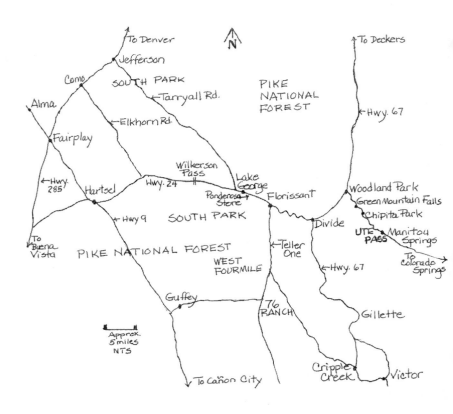

CHAPTER 1

THE BEGINNING

July 19, 1982, was one of many beautiful, sunny days in the Rocky Mountains of Colorado. At almost 9,000 feet elevation, the air was crisp as a snap of bubble wrap and clear as sparkling crystal. It was my 40th birthday, but there would be no party. I was alone in the rustic cabin that had been my home for twenty days. By then I had met a total of five people in Lake George, Colorado. Not only did no one know this was my birthday, hardly anyone knew me. I felt like a stranger in a foreign land. Reaching for a thread of familiarity – aside from furniture hauled from the east in a rental van – I latched onto, of all things, my old exercise routine: crunches, leg lifts, push-ups. A subtle reminder that I was still myself, though the surroundings were totally different.

In the upward thrust of a half-hearted leg lift, I started laughing out loud. Was I crazy to be in this middle-of-nowhere spot, embarking on a venture that screamed uncertainty? Red flags flew in my face like taunting monsters from a horror movie. What had driven a young woman who usually chose life's safe and secure paths into unknown territory with risks abounding and security nil? Laughter gave way to a moment of dry-mouthed panic and a temporary lapse into survival mentality. Was I out of my mind to think that taking home care and hospice services to the mountains was even possible? Would I be in over my head? Could I earn enough money to survive?

Early days in public health and hospice nursing, and later the challenges of providing rural home care and hospice services, tell a story of passion for the work I embraced and a love for the Colorado Rocky Mountains and its down-to-earth people. The territory where I chose to live and work spanned 2,000 square miles west of Pikes Peak. This sparsely populated area had a seductive draw, but not until later did I understand why. The people who called this piece of central Colorado home – many who were descendants of pioneers and ranching families – welcomed me and provided a safe haven as I traveled the back roads and ventured out in harsh weather, day and night, to visit patients in remote settings.

Aside from keeping memorable stories alive, documentation of the early days of rural hospice care in the United States gains historical significance as time goes by and hospice care evolves into its twenty-first century self. The heart of hospice's past is intricately woven into the concepts and approaches incorporated into today's delivery of this worthwhile service.

My experiences forming an agency and caring for patients are told as recalled from thirty-year-old memories and from accounts preserved in letters found in a dusty box while cleaning out my parents' basement. Often, these letters spilled out my last thoughts and frustrations as I unwound after a day of patient visits and a long evening of record keeping. My recollections and letters to Mom and Dad reveal hospice care and program development in the days when our country was just beginning to understand its value and significance.

Excerpts from letters are italicized. Patient names have been changed throughout the book. Names of local people who provided exceptional help and support in the early days have not been changed. They deserve recognition and gratitude. They were my earthly angels. Stepping into the unknown was a test of faith. Time after time I was reminded that God was leading me, looking out for me, and providing me with the stamina to keep going. I knew beyond a doubt that I had a full-time angel on my shoulder.

CHAPTER 2

HOSPICE CARE

Hospices have existed in other countries, primarily in Europe, since the Middle Ages, first as way stations for weary travelers, and later as hostels where dedicated nuns provided compassionate care for the sick and dying. The origin of the modern hospice movement is credited to Dame Cicely Saunders in England and later, in the United States, to Dr. Elisabeth Kubler-Ross, author of numerous books and other publications, including the classic, *On Death and Dying*.

Nowadays, many people have some knowledge of, if not a personal acquaintance with, hospice care. To date, several thousand hospices across the United States have helped millions of individuals and their loved ones wend their way through the ups and downs of final months, weeks, and days of life. Hospice's focus is on caring rather than curing, when cure is not a likely outcome. Comfort – physical, emotional, and spiritual – is the ultimate goal. Aggressive medical intervention is replaced with palliative care in the form of pain relief and symptom control, neither hastening nor prolonging the dying process.

The theory behind the modern hospice movement is that quite often, palliative care can be provided in a person's home by a team of compassionate volunteers and professionals from various caregiving disciplines – medical, nursing, therapies, and counseling. Living out one's last days at home offers the comfort of familiar surroundings and closeness of family and friends, even young children and pets, all of whom play an important role in the caregiving process and serve to enhance final days. When home care is not an option, inpatient hospices exist in many communities to provide the same kind of compassionate care.

In the late 1970's and early 1980's hospices were emerging across the United States. Cities and towns had adequate populations, resources, and support services to enable hospice programs to survive and succeed. Rural hospice development, on the other hand, was a chapter waiting to be written.

"You are starting a *what?*" was a frequent question when I moved to the central Colorado mountains in 1982 to begin hospice and home care nursing. "What is hospice?" I was asked more than once. Even the pronunciation of the word was in question. Would a ho-spice, spoken with a long "o" and a long "i," be a Spanish restaurant? For many in the area the idea had some appeal, but few people really wanted to talk about, or even think about, dying. After all, mountain people were survivors, tough and hardy folks who took risks and beat the odds. To them dying at home revived memories of Grandpa laid out in a homemade casket in the dining room, children being marched forward, one by one, to kiss a cold, pale cheek, with bad smells abounding. Not a pleasant experience. Could the "new" dying at home be any different, they wondered? Could it be better than drawing one's final breath in a hospital with the innovations that current medical technology had to offer?

Hospitals had a bad reputation among mountain folks, especially the elderly, who told me that being admitted to a hospital was like walking through death's door. You went in, they said, but more often than not, you didn't come out. Indeed, hospitals offered care and services that were appropriate for some dying patients, but I knew that many others could be managed at home if that was their preference *and* if support services were available to make that a viable option. My intention was to convince some key players that it could be done. New programs brought in by new people were often suspect in the eyes of rural folks, so I would have to defy that assumption and build credibility as well as trust.

Traveling to visit potential patients in their homes, presenting talks to community groups, and communicating the essence of this idea to anyone who would listen was my marketing plan. I distributed business cards and brochures. Every contact was a possible supporter and advocate. Nevertheless, even so much as discussing the subject of dying was distasteful to some people. I might as well have been selling caskets. "Why would anyone want to work with dying people?" I was asked. And then in the next breath, "Isn't that depressing?" I suppose those were obvious questions, but any hospice nurse would say without hesitation that this is a special kind of nursing that is inspiring, challenging, thought-provoking, educational, and at times sad — but definitely not depressing. In-home care, culminating in a home death, comprises the majority of hospice experiences. It is not for everyone, either as patient or caregiver, nor is it the calling of most nurses. Some nurses thrive on the action of the emergency room; some like bringing lives into the world; others are challenged by the highly technical environment of the operating room or the intensive care unit. My own niche was in the home setting, where patients and families could be themselves without the inevitable stress of a hospital experience. For nurses and other hospice workers, home care provides opportunities to be creative and to solve problems in ingenious ways without relying on hospital equipment and technology.

In addition to the physical care aspect, hospice nursing consists of more counseling, teaching, and advising than in most other nursing specialties. A hospice nurse steps into a family's world and, by being sensitive and perceptive, is able to mesh with their dynamic: their unique ways of functioning. Never overbearing, a nurse guides the family through their caregiving experience, shoring up their strengths and abilities and supplementing areas in which assistance is needed. As supporter, encourager, and listener, the nurse becomes a trustworthy confidant with whom the patient and family feel comfortable expressing the array of emotions that are sure to spill forth in the days, weeks, or months of their journey together.

Every home situation is different, each with its unique set of problems and all changing from one day to the next. A goal of hospice care is to enable a family or other caregiver(s) to experience a loved one's death feeling that everything possible in the continuum of compassionate care has been done, through their own and other caregivers' efforts. Having accomplished this task, they can grieve well, meaning that there will be no guilt or "should-haves" or "wish-we-hads." And no unfinished business. Strained relationships can be strengthened in final weeks and days. Memorable moments can be shared.

For many family caregivers, their hospice experience is a priceless gift. For hospice workers, being part of a family's unfolding story and being invited into their world is a privilege and an honor. Helping someone exit an earthly life peacefully and at the same time guiding a family as they prepare to say goodbye – to have those important conversations and to focus on the passage at hand – is ultimately rewarding. The ebbing of life as a body shuts down is indeed a momentous process, neither frightening nor as dramatic as usually depicted on television. It is an important part of life.

During my years of hospice nursing, not only did I learn about death and dying but also about life itself, as experience upon experience evolved into wisdom pertinent for all who are observing from the sidelines and wondering how their own lives might play out. The ensuing pages contain insights gleaned while caring for memorable patients and families, insights potentially relevant for those of us whose stories are still unfolding.

CHAPTER 3

Public Health Nursing

So how did a young woman from the Washington, DC suburbs – indoctrinated into eastern proprieties as espoused by Emily Post – make a giant geographical and cultural leap to mountain living? Hardly an impulsive move, the idea had been smoldering for years, surfacing during nursing school as a distinct pull away from hospital nursing, which in the mid-1960's, was the principal component of nursing education.

This leaning became apparent during the final assignment in the senior year of my baccalaureate nursing program: public health clinical practice. The locale to which I was assigned was intended for students who had their own transportation. Too few of us had cars that semester, and one outlying area was left to be filled. I must have drawn the short straw. Lack of a vehicle necessitated a ride on the city bus to the end of the line on the outskirts of Greensboro, North Carolina, then a one-mile walk on a dirt road to reach the patients I was to visit.

Outfitted in a student nurse's uniform – a dark blue dress with white collar and cuffs starched like cardboard – and toting a black leather nursing bag loaded with supplies and patient records, I hiked to their homes. By semester's end I sported the sleeve lines and V-neck of a farmer's tan and had worn holes in the soles of my loafers. In spite of the trekking, being "out in the field" and making home visits to patients with various health concerns was a kind of nursing that I liked. Prior to that semester we students had worked in all departments in the hospital. While my classmates were deciding which nursing specialty they would choose after graduation, I was at a loss because I liked it all – medicine, surgery, pediatrics, obstetrics, psychiatry. So public health, which included all of these areas, appealed to me. And I relished the sense of freedom and independence it conveyed.

My assignment was in a district that was home to a concentration of profoundly hearing impaired people who worked in the area's textile mills, unaffected by the racket of the mill machinery. Young deaf and mute parents learning to care for their newborn daughter fascinated me with their ingenious adaptations. A string tied from the infant's big toe to the sleeping mother's hand awakened her if the baby stirred at night. To speed their communication with each other, the couple had developed a shorthand version of sign language, some of which I learned and used with them. Otherwise we wrote notes back and forth.

Another patient was an elderly, mentally retarded diabetic lady (who called her disease the "sugar bedeedees") living alone in a wooded area in a rather unique structure – a shack made of discarded doors of assorted colors, lined up and attached to each other to form a small one-room dwelling. She had no electricity or running water, and she used a potbellied wood stove to cook her meals and heat her little abode in winter. Her outhouse, standing like a guard shack over a hole in the ground was a discarded antique red telephone booth – the kind with chicken wire embedded in the clear glass windows and folding door. She was a picture of contentment, though a diabetic diet was far beyond her level of comprehension.

A final visit of my day of walking from home to home was saved for a chronic lung disease patient who needed weekly assessment of his condition. We students carried no monitoring equipment with us in those days other than a stethoscope and blood pressure apparatus, but we were taught to observe for symptoms of oxygen depletion or a worsening condition and to use nursing judgment in evaluating our patients, a skill that served me well in years to come. This elderly man felt sorry for me, having to walk so far to see him, so at the end of a visit he hooked up his portable oxygen and drove me over rutted roads to the bus stop in his ancient, rattling pickup truck. I was in my element – outdoors, free from the confines of a hospital, and working with a variety of patient problems. A decision to pursue a public health nursing career was a given.

* * *

Returning home to Northern Virginia, I was hired as a public health nurse in Fairfax County, which in the 1960's bore no resemblance to its present image of urban affluence. Fifty years ago, in spite of its being a Washington,

DC suburb, the county was dotted with poverty pockets, including rural areas that lacked indoor plumbing, electricity and water. My initial month of orientation was south of DC in the vicinity of U.S. Route 1, the primary southern access to the city prior to the construction of Interstate 95.

One particularly vivid memory was a home visit made in a rather unusual poverty-ridden settlement, a notorious landmark with a longtime existence in southern Fairfax County. My assignment was to assess a newborn in this small enclave of indigent black families. And yes, in 1964 areas segregated by color were still prevalent. This particular housing, far from acceptable by anyone's standards, was a sad commentary on what was permitted (or overlooked) at the time. The homes were run-down, unpainted duplex shacks situated around a communal water spigot protruding from the ground. Derelict outhouses stood behind the dwellings. Electricity was nonexistent. Even in broad daylight, the interiors of the sparsely furnished homes were dim, with only a small window or two, without glass or screens, providing light and at the same time welcoming flies.

There I was, fledgling public health nurse, trying to do an infant examination on a dark-skinned baby in an unlit room. We weighed babies in a cloth diaper sling, knotted at diagonal corners and tied to scales that were a miniature version of those used in a meat market or for weighing fish. I had to use my flashlight to read the weight and then do the infant assessment. Though I knew the surroundings were not ideally conducive to the baby's health, the environment was not dangerous, and this wasn't the first baby to have lived there.

Nurses were never to indicate, verbally or non-verbally, anything less than acceptance of the people encountered, regardless of appalling conditions, obnoxious smells, or anything that might be offensive. If conditions were unsafe, steps – sometimes legal – had to be taken to ensure that basic needs would be met. Even in that unfortunate case, a nurse needed to be able to connect with people at their level of functioning and establish rapport in order to work with them. I was learning to welcome the challenge of dealing with a variety of health problems, many in less than ideal circumstances, and hoped that my attempts at teaching and counseling might have even a slight impact.

Motels known as tourist courts, bypassed by Interstate 95, had fallen into disrepair and had become home to transients and indigent families who rented rooms by the week, unable to accumulate a month's rent for better quarters. Included in this population were tuberculosis patients who needed monitoring and guidance related to compliance with medication regimens and medical care. There were young families with child health concerns, such as care of frail newborns and management of handicapping conditions. Chronic illness in adults was prevalent — heart failure, lung disease, and diabetes. These people were barely able to meet basic survival needs, much less cope with health challenges. It was both eye-opening and sad to see people living in such marginal conditions, especially when, just a few miles distant, were lavish homes of wealthy suburbanites.

Around that time, I began to grasp the concept of "dysfunctional families," usually adults who opted for behavior choices detrimental to their health and often to the wellbeing of their children. Cigarettes and alcohol often trumped food. Frustrations with life escalated into angry exchanges and sometimes progressed to domestic violence, neglect, or desertion. Lacking effective problem-solving skills, these people lived a day-to-day, crisis-oriented existence. Understandably, these struggling families often failed to follow through on a nurse's teaching and counseling efforts. In attempts to deal with the challenges and frustrations of working with dysfunctional families, one basic public health nursing tenet prevailed: to accept the integrity of the individual and avoid judging or criticizing, acknowledging that regardless of the behavior exhibited, it was the best choice that an individual was capable of making at a given time. Not that poor decisions were excused, but at least they were understood. Application of this concept enabled me to be effective in difficult family situations and to minimize my own frustrations when recommendations were not followed.

The Fairfax County Health Department was ahead of the times, already providing a home care program when Medicare was enacted in 1965. Public health nurses visited homebound patients needing hands-on nursing care as well as management of unstable medical conditions. With the advent of Medicare, the home care program became "certified," meaning that the health department could – of all the unheard of things at the time – charge a fee for home visits to patients who met Medicare criteria, thereby generating revenue for the program. Prior to that, all health department services were provided free of charge to the public.

As my career advanced, I went to graduate school for a master's degree in public health nursing administration and in several years was overseeing the home care program. Being in this mid-level management position meant that I was no longer out in the field seeing patients but instead, was in the office advising and supervising staff nurses. I missed my early days as a public health nurse, dealing with health problems in home settings.

One January day I stared out of my office window at the winter-gray Northern Virginia sky until whatever I was supposed to be working on drew me back to reality. Though the scenery was limited to the high-rise county governmental office building next door, a floor-to-ceiling expanse of glass provided an inescapable invitation to distraction. That small office was my abode for eight hours a day unless a meeting intervened or, better yet, an opportunity to go home visiting with one of the staff nurses. Program planning, budgeting and other administrative duties sidelined me from the nursing career I loved.

The state had sent me to graduate school to learn management skills, but directing the work of other nurses was not producing the satisfaction I derived from caregiving, counseling, and patient teaching. Program administration was indeed challenging, but not the challenge that excited or sustained me. I felt guilty, even ungrateful, reckoning with growing boredom in a secure, well-paying nursing position. More than one jaw dropped when, on a lousy day at work, I boldly admitted to a room full of nurses that my career goal was to return to staff level nursing. I longed for life outside the concrete box.

Along with dissatisfaction with work came an itch to relocate. By the mid-1970's, traffic, noise, air pollution, and a burgeoning population in Fairfax County had driven me to the outskirts of the county. I was divorced and living a bucolic existence with my daughter Leigh Anne on five wooded acres 35 miles southwest of the District of Columbia. The property was sufficiently remote to have been the site of a former moonshine operation, with broken jars, copper pipe, and other equipment remaining as evidence of illegal liquor production. Neighbors on either side were distantly visible, but only in winter, when the towering oaks were bare. We heated the house with our abundant supply of firewood and ate vegetables from a large garden. My *Bon Appetit* subscription had been replaced with *Organic Gardening*, and I learned to use a chain saw and a rototiller. Even living in such serene surroundings, I continued to wish for a career change and considered a possible move from the DC area. But where?

During childhood I enjoyed our family's summer trips to Southwest Virginia to visit the elderly aunt and uncle who had raised my father. Dad's roots were in this part of Appalachia, so our visits were steeped in family history and tales of mountain life. Aunt Alpha and Uncle George's little four-room clapboard house barely accommodated our family of five. One sister and I slept on a single bed in the living room beside a coal heater. A lush garden behind the house produced the best vegetables I had ever eaten, transformed into feasts by Aunt Alpha on an old, wood-fired cook stove. To cross the New River at the end of their dirt road, a yank on a bell cord summoned an elderly man who slowly emerged from his house and poled a creaking wooden raft from one side of the river to the other. Bouncing up the hills and down into the "hollers" in the old Model A Ford with Uncle

George behind the wheel was nothing short of pure fun. We visited relatives who lived up rutted mountain roads and lacked indoor plumbing, telephones, and electricity, as well as teeth. What characters they were! My city-girl eyes were wide open. I loved that mountain country.

In contemplating relocation, Southwest Virginia came to mind, though such a move would be unreasonable, if not impossible, until after Leigh Anne's graduation from high school in five years. I dared not move her from the proximity of friends and family in suburbia to the heart of Appalachia. My idea of a better life most certainly would not be hers.

At a health department meeting downstate, I had met a lady who was the lone public health nurse assigned to a Southwest Virginia county. She did everything – home care, child health clinics, and home visits for nursing supervision of all kinds of health concerns – a true generalist and just what I had in mind. She anticipated retiring in several years, and I entertained the possibility of acquiring her position, tromping the hills and hollows, back to the kind of nursing I loved. A transfer within the state system would leave my retirement, health insurance, and other benefits intact. So there it was – a well-designed plan that would keep me going for the time being. At least until another plan emerged.

CHAPTER 4

CHANGE OF PLANS

Into my life entered a high school classmate with whom I had become acquainted following our twentieth reunion. He remembered me as the girl who had won the science fair. I remembered him not at all. He seemed like a nice guy, and he happened to work in a place that aroused my interest — Denver, Colorado.

I had grown up hearing about Colorado from my parents' stories about a big ranch in that far-off state out west where they had visited some of Dad's relatives. The beautiful piece of pink granite they had found on Pikes Peak went with me to Show-and-Tell in first grade. Their descriptions of the old ranch – real cowboys herding cattle on their horses, the long dining table piled with food where unmannered ranch hands came in each noon for a sumptuous meal, the old bunkhouse where they stayed – all stirred my childhood imagination. Was there really a place where mountain snow never melted and sky was bluer than a robin's egg? When, as fifth graders, we each chose a state to write a report on, mine was Colorado.

Seven years later, as a high school senior, I was fortunate to have been part of an exchange trip to Lakewood High School in the Denver suburbs. For two glorious weeks in the fall of 1959, our group was treated to a sample of western life and to a world that I had only heard about and seen through my parents' photographs and souvenirs. We toured Denver and the state capitol, visited the newly opened Air Force Academy in Colorado Springs, tobogganed at Loveland Ski Basin, drove around Golden with its School of Mines and Coors Brewery, and saw the Face on the Bar Room Floor in Central City. We attended classes at Lakewood High School and returned home sporting Stetson hats. I loved every minute of it, and my eyes were opened to a whole new world.

In the summer of 1981, encouraged by my high school classmate, I visited Denver once again and had a delightful reunion with the exchange student in whose home I had stayed. Twenty-one years of correspondence had kept us connected. During a conversation about my desire to leave Northern Virginia, she encouraged me to consider moving to Denver. For the second time in my life, I loved Colorado – so much so that I returned to Virginia with a new plan, one in which every piece fell into place. My exchange student offered a rental house in the Denver suburbs for Leigh Anne and me. My seatmate on the return flight from Denver to DC suggested a job possibility in public health. Hearing of my intent to relocate, a health department co-worker arranged to rent my Virginia house.

My resignation from that secure, salaried position with its many benefits, as well as years paid into a retirement system, was effective in thirty days. I was saying good-bye to all of it. Health department nurses were flabbergasted. My parents were horrified. Leigh Anne thought her life was over. Mine was just beginning. I packed my belongings, arranged for a moving van, parked Leigh Anne with my parents until school started, and headed for Colorado.

CHAPTER 5

Denver Hospice

For almost a year I lived in the Denver suburbs. My transplanted fourteen-year-old daughter adapted well to her junior high school and made new friends. An ad for a part-time nursing position at Hospice of Metro Denver (now The Denver Hospice) drew my attention. Not that I knew much about hospice nursing, but I liked the concept of caring for people who chose to die at home. And I would be back in my niche, doing home care. I wanted to try it, but I had a major deficiency in experience: I had never even seen anyone die, much less taken care of a dying patient.

The summer between high school and nursing school when I worked as a nurse's aide at our local hospital, I helped a nurse prepare the body of a deceased patient for transfer to the morgue – toes and fingers tagged, eyes closed, cold and jaundiced body wrapped in a sheet. Pretty gruesome, I thought at the time. Then in my junior year in nursing school, my pediatric case study patient died of leukemia. I wasn't on duty when he died, but went up to the pediatric unit that night to visit his grief-stricken parents as they sat with their son's lifeless body. That was it – my entire experience with death. Though I had been a nurse for some fifteen years, my career in public health was geared to the prevention of disease and death – the other end of the spectrum. I wasn't even sure that I would be hired as a hospice nurse, but I applied for the position anyway.

I had learned a bit about hospice care for the terminally ill as the health department's representative on the advisory board of the newly formed Hospice of Northern Virginia in 1981, but that was only for a very brief time before I left the area. My interest and desire must have overridden my lack of experience, as Hospice of Metro Denver hired me and walked me through the basics of hospice nursing. The experienced nurses were a tremendous help to their new recruit, who was totally ignorant of so many aspects of hospice care.

I caught on quickly, however, and thrived on the challenge of providing nursing care, comfort and compassion to people living out their final weeks, days and hours at home. Without the monitoring equipment and resources that are readily available in a hospital setting, the home environment offered untold opportunities for creative problem solving with little to go on but knowledge, experience (sorely lacking at that point), and intuition. I liked the family-centered approach, which was also the backbone of public health nursing.

In home settings, the family is the patient as well as the person with the "patient" designation. "Family" is a term used loosely and is whomever the patient identifies as family, not always people related by blood or marriage. The scene often entails emotional struggles and conflicts. When people are on their own turf, they are comfortable being themselves, warts and all. From public health nursing experience I was used to dealing with family interaction, however it presented.

Hospice nurses provide patients and caregivers with anticipatory guidance as to what the dying process will entail and also teach them how to care for a dying person. Pain management was new to me. I learned narcotics dosages, how to balance pain relief with side effects, and the use of other medications and interventions to enhance the effectiveness of drugs in providing a tolerable level of comfort for the patient without over-sedation. With that important goal achieved, the patient and family could make the most of their remaining time together.

My initial experience with a home death occurred during the first weekend that I was the on-call nurse. Although we were assigned to geographical areas, weekend call duty covered the entire Denver metropolitan area. The answering service paged me on a Saturday evening, and I phoned the family for a report on the patient and directions to the home. I'll admit to having had a case of the jitters, driving to an unfamiliar patient in an unfamiliar part of Denver at about 10:00 p.m. Would I remember everything I was supposed to do? Would the family be able to tell that I was new at this? Then I quieted my nervous mind. This was not about me. I prayed that I would be able to help this patient to be comfortable as life ended and the family to be comforted through the experience. Amen.

I found the address easily and stepped in to do whatever I could to ease a person's passage. A barely responsive lady lay in her bed. The scene was quiet and peaceful. Her life was ebbing and, in hospice vernacular, death was imminent. The patient, surrounded by family, was breathing noisily and irregularly and fidgeting with the bedding – all signs of impending death. As confident as I could be with what I had learned so far, I explained , to the family what was happening and assured them that they were witnessing a normal part of the dying process. As we sat together, the adult children reminisced about their mother's life. They were calm in their acceptance of the passage that was in progress and thankful to have had their mother at home during her illness.

Several hours later the patient breathed a final breath. The event transpired as I expected, with no surprises for the family (or me). As was our hospice custom, I prepared the body for the family's final time with her and stayed until the mortuary had taken her from the home. The family was grateful for support from hospice during the previous months and especially to have had a nurse with them at the time of their mother's death. So it was – my first home death – a textbook example of a peaceful end to life and reassurance for me that I could be a competent hospice nurse.

With Leigh Anne back in Virginia visiting her father and grandparents for the Christmas holiday, I was alone with no plans, so I volunteered to be on call on Christmas Day. Knowing that dying people often muster the will to live through a holiday or a family event, I expected a quiet day. But a call did come in from the answering service, not for a home death but for a new patient. That was hardly what I expected. A visiting relative who was familiar with hospice care had convinced her sister, diagnosed with advanced kidney cancer, to call for our services. I visited the patient, her partner, and the visiting sister. As was routine on a first visit, I explained the hospice concept and home care services. The patient, lying in a hospital bed and obviously quite ill, stated with all certainty that this was not for her because she was not dying. Both her partner and sister rolled their eyes and otherwise conveyed their disbelief. Knowing that renal cancer was generally fatal (at least in 1981) and figuring that this patient was at a stage of denying the inevitable, I proceeded to acknowledge her feelings, reinforcing the importance of hope, belief, and so on.

I visited this lady many times during the ensuing months, as she happened to live in my assigned area. Her devoted partner took a leave of absence from work and provided excellent care, including sleeping on the floor beside the hospital bed in order to respond to calls during the night. The patient was right. She did not die. Her physician pronounced the disappearance of the tumor "a miracle," and this determined lady was eventually discharged from hospice care. Sometimes the will to live surpasses all prognoses. No one knows when a life will end, and it never hurts to listen to the patient. Miracles *do* happen.

Another referral was for a man who had seen his physician for a chronic cough and had been diagnosed earlier that day with lung cancer. This man had decided not to pursue any of the treatment options offered, so his doctor referred him to hospice. Admitting a patient before the end stage of illness was helpful, in that it allowed time to establish a close relationship with the patient and family. I phoned the home and talked to the patient's wife, who related that her husband's condition was stable and not causing him discomfort or her any care problems. She was receptive to having hospice services, and we decided that I would visit the following day. She called the next morning to report that her husband had died in his sleep sometime during the night. She believed that hearing the diagnosis and prognosis convinced him that he was in for an experience in which he did not want to participate. His solution was to spare himself and his family the difficult time ahead and check out. The will to live, or not, is indeed powerful.

Receiving a diagnosis of a fatal or life-threatening illness is an instant life changer. More often than not it is the beginning of an unwanted roller coaster ride – ups and downs of exhausting duration. Lives are interrupted. Plans go out the window. People are cheated out of retirement years and time with family. Grieving begins when disbelief gives way to reality and the pending loss is realized. Many unknowns complicate a devastating situation, as choices are considered and decisions made.

The field of medicine has a curing focus. Physicians are very good at using the knowledge, skill, and ammunition at their disposal to wage war on a disease process. Sometimes the treatment is more than a body can withstand. Quality-of-life questions prevail: whether to pursue aggressive treatment or not, and then, if intervention is not producing desired results, when to stop. Disagreement among family members may add stress to an already stressful situation. I believe that a patient's wishes are paramount and should be expressed, talked about, and respected without imposing a burden of guilt on a person who is dealing with a life-threatening illness.

Ending treatment does not equate giving up hope, whether it is hope for a miracle or simply hope for a pain-free day.

Fear may preclude rational thinking. Asking "What is the worst that can happen?" or "What are you the most afraid of?" may help a person get in touch with fears. Often someone will realize that he or she has no control over what is feared and that lying awake at night rehearsing possible events is counterproductive. When the worst-case scenario is death, that possibility needs to be acknowledged. Further discussion with family may include "What will you do then?" and other questions that are thought provoking and deal with eventualities. Talking through these fears helps people identify and focus on issues that need their attention rather than letting an unbridled brain take over.

Support from friends and relatives during the disease process is so very important, even though avoidance of an uncomfortable situation may be tempting. Not that people intend to ignore their friends at a difficult time, but their own discomfort with tears and sadness may preclude stepping in. Simply being there is far more important than knowing exactly what to say or what to do. That said, trying to come across as knowing how another person feels is inappropriate because no one can be that perceptive or intuitive. It is better to convey the truth with empathy as in, "I can't imagine how you feel. This must be just awful for you." Being with a crying person may be unsettling, but an excellent piece of advice given in hospice orientation is to look through the tears, to accept tears as simply a necessary expression of emotion. Crying along with the patient and family is both okay and understandable. These are sad situations that warrant tears. The patient and family need shoulders to lean on and listeners with whom they feel safe expressing their feelings and anxieties. Being able to extend compassion comes from within and is a genuine gift of self.

* * *

An interesting on-call visit was my first to a family of a culture other than my own. I arrived at the home to find a living room crowded with family and friends, all laughing and talking in an almost party-like atmosphere. Was I at the right place? I wondered. I introduced myself and was directed down a narrow hall to a back bedroom where the patient, a frail elderly man, lay quietly in his bed. He was alone. His breathing pattern indicated that I had arrived none too soon for this family's home death experience. After a brief search I located the patient's wife in the kitchen, stirring a pot of soup. As gently as possible, I told her that I suspected her husband to be very close to death, thinking that she would want to be by his side. She matter of factly said, "I thought so," and continued stirring the soup. Hmmm. This was not what I expected. I asked the visitors if anyone wanted to be with the patient as his life ended. Having no takers, I returned to the bedroom, stood at the bedside, and held this man's shriveled hand, taking a breath along with each of his raspy, waning ones. After a few moments I said, "George, I think this is it for you. Are you ready to go?" And with one big sigh, he died. As if responding to suggestion, he breathed no more. Even as I announced his passing to family and friends, no one went to the bedside, and the socializing continued without missing a beat.

For certain, no two deaths are the same, and each family deals with dying in its own way. To be effective in these situations, the nurse needs to connect with and become part of each family's experience in whatever context it evolves. Expectations and preconceived ideas go out the window.

* * *

Religious beliefs, or the absence of them, often play a part in the lives of people who are approaching death. At times, spiritual issues surface when nurses or other hospice workers are with a patient, particularly when he or she conveys a fear of dying or questions his or her religious beliefs. Hospice programs offer spiritual counseling, but when a family has a relationship with clergy or another spiritual leader, they often prefer to call on someone whom they already know. However accomplished, addressing spiritual issues is important in order for a person nearing death to come to some resolution of fears or guilt or worries or whatever is occupying his or her mind.

At one point I had two patients, one who ascribed to no particular religion and one who had been a devout, practicing Roman Catholic his entire life. Patient number one was at peace with the impending outcome, saying that he was not afraid of dying and was comforted in knowing that he had lived a good life, had no regrets, and was ready for the end to come. He said he was prepared to go to whatever better place was waiting for him.

As we talked, I thought to myself how wonderful it was that someone could feel so positive about the life he had lived. I wished I could have known him in earlier times.

Patient number two, on the other hand, was the embodiment of fear, much to the distress of his wife, who could not understand her husband's anxiety. On one wall of the bedroom was a painting of Jesus; on another, a photograph of the Pope; and in his pajama pocket, a small statue of the Virgin Mary, which he occasionally reached for and held in a weak hand. He openly expressed fear that he had not met the mark to ensure his passage to heaven. His priest had visited several times and was unable to calm this man's fears. I felt sad that he was in such a distraught state of mind and that his religion had not been a source of comfort to him in his final days.

Beginning with my Denver hospice experience I became interested in the role that religion or spirituality plays as a patient nears the end of life on earth. A religious past, or lack of one, does not necessarily dictate a person's spiritual experience as life ebbs. Nevertheless, dying has spiritual implications for most people, even the avowed agnostic, who expresses anger toward a God he does not acknowledge. Or, on the other hand, sees death as an affirmation that there is no God. People who have no belief in an afterlife may search for a spiritual connection near the end. Whereas others, who have a strong belief system and faith that has sustained them through life's ups and downs, generally tend to exit this life with peace, confident that a better place awaits them. Even those of strong faith, both patients and families, may question God or express anger toward a God who allows pain and suffering. Accepting that the "why" truly has no plausible answer is one step in moving toward resolution of a situation that may seem so very unfair and unde-served. The truth is, bad things do happen, and life is far from fair. Lives are snuffed out in their prime. Families are deprived of their loved ones. The world around us is over-filled with suffering. All of us would be well advised to appreciate every good day that we can share with those we love and to reach out in empathy to those around us who are dealing with loss and grief.

The death of a man I'll call Bob taught me an impor-tant lesson. Bob had lung cancer that had metastasized to his spine. His bone pain was severe. An avid outdoors-man, Bob had enjoyed a lengthy and successful career with the Forest Service. His wife pointed to the picture on the mantel of the handsome, strapping man that he had been before cancer ravaged his body and reduced this strong sixty-four-year-old to an emaciated figure lying in bed, writhing in pain. And dying.

Pain management was a priority and a challenge. In addition to the narcotics ordered for his pain, his wife and I worked out a plan that included relaxation meth-ods and medication to relieve his anxiety. This was one patient whose period of imminent death – usually 24 to 72 hours – was seemingly endless, probably due to his having been in excellent physical condition prior to his illness. Bob's devoted wife, clad in her nightgown, lay next to her barely responsive husband for nearly a week. Their three daughters were in the bedroom more often than not. Moments of laughter as well as tears enhanced their togetherness, as they talked of past adventures. The scene was a touching tribute to a much loved husband and father. Finally, and peacefully, death did come.

Mixed with a family's sadness is an array of feelings and emotions – often thankfulness, even joy, odd as it sounds, that a loved one "has gone to a better place," whatever that means in their belief system. There is frequently pride from having accomplished a task that at times was exhausting and may have seemed insurmountable. And understandable relief that a huge and difficult job is finished. Because of their involvement in the care of their loved one, and because they are prepared for the dying process, hospice families are often at a stage of peace and acceptance, not wishing for suffering to continue and as ready as they can be to let go and say goodbye. No matter how well prepared they are, however, they still have to come to grips with the finality of death. The breath that doesn't happen. The pallor that follows. A hospice nurse sits with a family while they process the event that has occurred. They may talk through it, often tearfully. They may make phone calls. They may make a pot of coffee. They decide when to call the mortuary. There is no hurry. The time is theirs.

I made several additional visits to Bob's wife, with whom I had developed a special relationship during our many visits, before a bereavement volunteer was assigned. We looked at family pictures from years past. During Bob's career as a forest ranger, they had lived in various scenic, though isolated, places and had amassed volumes of unforgettable experiences. With a wistful, far-off look, Bob's wife said, "I am so thankful for everything we did when we thought we couldn't afford it," and as an afterthought, "or shouldn't have done it for one reason or another."

That statement has been with me ever since and has been a piece of wisdom that has influenced my own life. With that thought in mind, I pondered my desire to take this kind of nursing to the mountains. Denver was and is a great city, and Hospice of Metro Denver, an excellent training ground. But quite simply – I was not a city girl. Somehow, in spite of my suburban upbringing, a bit of country rumbled below the surface.

CHAPTER 6

EXPLORING

How well I remember the day in early October when the mountains west of Denver had made an overnight transformation from gray-brown to white. The snowy peaks stood in stark contrast to the bluest of skies and the bright school-bus gold of the aspen trees. I wanted to be in those mountains, caring for patients in their homes. But where? And how?

On my two days off each week I began exploring. I wanted to know the Colorado that was out there waiting for me to discover and to find out if my mountain-nurse idea might ever become a reality. My wanderings always gravitated westward toward the majestic mountains that dwarfed anything that lay below. Unlike the soft greens and blue haze of the mountains in the east, these massive peaks rising sharply above timberline spoke grandeur in a different language. The mere sight of such formidable monoliths fueled an adrenaline rush in this transplanted easterner.

One beautiful blue-sky day I traveled south from Denver to Colorado Springs and then west on U.S. Highway 24. The view a short distance to the north encompassed Garden of the Gods, a place my parents had fond memories of, and was indeed the beautiful array of red rocks they had described. The first town situated off of the highway was Manitou Springs, known for its historically sacred waters frequented by Indian tribes and later, as a resort town picturesquely nestled at the base of 14,110-foot Pikes Peak.

From there the highway began a snaking climb up Ute Pass* following Fountain Creek. Towering rock faces graced the sides of this chasm carved millions of years ago by glaciers and the resulting movement of rocks and water toward lower ground. Ute Pass, originally Ute Trail, was an Indian footpath and an animal trail long before being traversed by mountain explorers. Later widened into a wagon road, it was heavily used as the main route for transporting miners and supplies to Colorado's gold fields farther west. Further widening and realignment in 1872 enabled its use by stage coaches traveling west from Colorado Springs. In the late 1800's the Colorado Midland Railroad climbed Ute Pass, and finally, in 1939, U.S. Highway 24 opened and followed approximately the same route along the north side of Pikes Peak.

Little settlements along the way, including turn-of-the-century resort towns of Chipita Park and Green Mountain Falls, appeared to be relics from the past with a preponderance of log cabins perched on steep hillsides. Farther up the Pass was Woodland Park, a picturesque town reminiscent of the Old West, with its boardwalk,

---

* A "pass" is a travel route through mountains and is usually a crossing at a "saddle" or gap that avoids climbing over the top of a mountain.

bar, and false-front shops. Cabins sided with log slabs spoke of past lumbering operations in the area. West of Woodland Park the old ranching community of Divide came into view. At 9,198 feet, the highest point on the Pass, it is the diversion point for streams trickling east toward the Arkansas River and west to the South Platte River. It is the junction of Highway 67 which goes south to Cripple Creek and on to Victor.

Continuing west, Highway 24 winds through Florissant Canyon and emerges thirty-five miles west of Colorado Springs at Florissant, a spot in the road consisting of several old buildings, a mercantile, gas station, and post office. The area encompasses an enormous ancient lake bed formed from prehistoric volcanic activity and surrounded by long-dormant volcanoes. As the ash from the volcanoes settled and built up, it formed what is now the petrified forest of Florissant Fossil Beds National Monument, replete with fossilized plants and creatures of the past. In the gold mining era, the latter part of the 1800's, Florissant was a major railroad depot and shipping point for prospectors, mail, and supplies going south on the road now known as Teller One, to the lucrative Cripple Creek Mining District via the stage line.

Six miles west of Florissant was Lake George, another collection of old buildings including a restaurant, post office, fire station, and garage – all small. The picturesque lake for which the area was named supplied ice blocks for refrigeration in past years. An unpaved road to the south followed the Platte River's course through the beautiful rock-sided Eleven-Mile Canyon.

From Lake George, Highway 24 led to Wilkerson Pass at an altitude of 9,507 feet. The breathtaking 180-degree view from the top of the Pass across the expanse of South Park to the snowcapped Collegiate Peaks of the Sawatch Range was (and still is) the most awe-inspiring scene my eyes had ever beheld. I couldn't get enough of this enticing environment, so I returned the next week and weeks following. I felt an unmistakable draw to the Florissant area and wondered if I might pursue my dream of mountain nursing in this historical part of Colorado. Plenty of footwork and homework would be necessary in order to ascertain whether such an idea would be even remotely feasible.

Beginning in the winter of 1981-82, every week that weather permitted, I drove down to Colorado Springs and up Ute Pass to explore the territory that sparked my interest. Two counties, Teller and the southern section of Park, spanned the area I focused on. I learned that home care services were available in the eastern, most populous side of Teller County by a visiting nurse who lived in Woodland Park but worked for an agency in Colorado Springs. Farther west in Teller County and in all of South Park, home care was unavailable. Not surprisingly, no hospice programs existed in any part of the area.

Since there was not an existing agency to which I could attach myself, I concluded that I would have to go it alone and form an agency. It would be a monumental task, and not one I wanted to tackle. I already knew how much I disliked the administrative aspect of nursing service delivery. Did I really want to go there again? Was I crazy even to let such an idea enter my mind? Maybe. But I was sure of one thing: I wanted to take home care and hospice to the mountains, and there was only one way to do it. At that point, while self-satisfaction remained a strong motivator, I was beginning to adjust to the fact that I had uncovered a geographical area that lacked an element of health care that I was prepared to provide. I could offer a worthwhile service to the people who lived in this area. It was an opportunity that I couldn't turn my back on.

A nearly overwhelming amount of groundwork faced me, as if I were back in graduate school with an assignment of doing a community assessment and establishing a need for health services. Though this task seemed like an academic exercise, I was thankful that I knew how to do it. I gathered bits and pieces of information from anyone who would talk to me, in order to identify local resources (though few) that would support such an agency. Each contact led to another – the public health nurses in each county, the head nurse at the 16-bed hospital in Fairplay (whom I first encountered when she was mopping the floor), pharmacists and physicians in Woodland Park, and a local newspaper columnist.

Transportation to the Fairplay Hospital Emergency Room

I zeroed in on a 2,000-square-mile area that included Green Mountain Falls, Woodland Park, Divide, Cripple Creek, Victor, Florissant, Lake George, Guffey, Fairplay, Jefferson, and Alma – all small places and most with a mining history. Driving the unpaved back roads in an expanse surrounded by snowcapped mountains, I learned firsthand where the deer and the antelope played, as well as buffalo and elk. I had yet to hear a "discouraging word." The skies were definitely not cloudy, and cattle roamed free on the range. This was the west that I had only seen on television and in the movies. I was awestruck.

When I wasn't meeting people and checking out resources in Park and Teller Counties, I was back in Denver continuing to work for Hospice. My evenings were spent creating a unique agency on paper. It would be a combination hospice and home care program in which all staff would be trained as both home care and hospice care providers. Though a combined agency was not an acceptable idea at the time among hospice purists, especially when the same staff would serve both kinds of patients, I knew it to be the right decision for several reasons.

From my knowledge of hospice principles, I ascribed to the idea of helping people and their families live through life-threatening illnesses and the grief associated with a major loss. From past home care experience, I knew that these patients, too, were dealing with loss, whether recovering from a stroke, suffering the effects of congestive heart failure, or coping with any other debilitating condition that impacted their lives and ability to function. Home care workers needed to have a hospice mindset – meaning the knowledge and ability to be compassionate and to address loss and grief issues as well as anger and frustration that is often expressed by patients and families.   And in addition, I had seen that patients who had become attached to their home care workers did not want to terminate those personal relationships to receive care from a different agency – a hospice – if their condition deteriorated.   Finally, knowing that hospice patients would comprise the minority of the caseload in a rural area, a home care component would be necessary for the agency to survive financially.

Compliance with Colorado state hospice licensing standards and federal requirements to be dually certified as both a hospice and home care provider was a must in order to secure reimbursement for services from Medicare and Medicaid and eventually, private insurers. There was the necessary paperwork to become a not-for-profit Colorado corporation, obtaining 501(c) (3) status in order to apply for grants and other funding and for donations to be tax deductible. As I pounded out the required documentation and a policy and procedure manual on my little Smith-Corona portable typewriter, I convinced myself that this phase of agency development was but a necessary exercise and merely a means to an end, though most certainly the downside.

Having successfully met all state and Federal requirements, Prospect Home Care and Hospice was ready to begin offering services on July 1, 1982. The name "Prospect" reflected the mining history of the area. A prospect was a hoped for mine of gold or silver to be developed or explored. It also embodied the concept of anticipation, which so accurately reflected the inception of the agency as well as the state of mind of the patients and families that would be served. A prospector was the person doing the exploring, and I felt like that person.

CHAPTER 7

THE RANCH

Frequent letters kept my parents apprised of my activities and plans. Their interest grew beyond normal parental concern, to worry and suspicion that I was headed for a crisis. They had always been supportive of my endeavors, but in this case, their encouragement seemed rather guarded. I understood their skepticism. After all, I was swimming in uncharted waters, not exactly sure where I was going or what lay ahead. To divert their attention, my ramblings focused on positive aspects such as the beautiful scenery, wildlife sightings, and my travels within the area.

As I described my locale, they recognized place names such as Cripple Creek, Florissant, and Guffey and began to impart information about the old family ranch and my relatives who lived there. The more details I heard, the more I realized that the location of the 76 Ranch, south of Florissant in an area known as West Fourmile, was in the area that I intended to serve. My parents sent photographs taken on their 1939 and 1941 trips to the ranch and later, newspaper articles, letters, and other information about my relatives.

I learned that Laura Belle Carrico, my grandfather's first cousin, met John Witcher, a widower some twenty or so years her senior, in southwest Virginia where she was born and was residing at the time of their meeting. He had gone west to Colorado in 1860, first as a miner in the Fairplay area, then a farmer near Florence, and finally, a prosperous rancher, having secured the sprawling 76 Ranch in Teller and Park Counties in 1872. Several years after their meeting, Laura Carrico and John Witcher were married in Cripple Creek in 1905. While on a Christmas trip to Niagara Falls in 1910, John had a stroke and died a week later. Laura returned to the ranch she had grown to love and continued successfully managing the cattle ranching operations for the next 44 years, until her death at age 90.

As the story unfolded, I learned that my dad's Uncle Silas, brother of Uncle George, who had raised my father, had moved out to the ranch from southwest Virginia in 1910 when he was 23 years old. His cousin Laura had suggested that Colorado's clear, pure air might cure his tuberculosis. Silas Pinion assisted Laura in managing the ranch, served as president of the Farmer's Club, was active in local politics, and became a popular Teller County Commissioner. My parents had visited him and Laura in 1939 and had returned to the ranch in the fall of 1941 following his death to visit Laura and to see Uncle Silas's grave at Fourmile Cemetery. Their photos showed the ranch house where they stayed, my father and a ranch hand on horseback in front of the Fourmile Grange hall, scenes around the ranch, the view from Wilkerson Pass, and Uncle Silas's grave.

Silas Pinion at the 76 Ranch, 1939

As I pressed Mom and Dad for 40-year-old memories about the ranch and the surrounding area, the rest of the story surfaced. They had always believed that it was on their 1941 trip, in their upstairs bedroom at the ranch house, that an egg and sperm collided to become me. Though I greeted the world in Washington, DC, my life had more than likely begun on the 76 Ranch in Florissant, Colorado. That surprising revelation both explained and justified my affinity for the area. I knew beyond a doubt that I had discovered the place where I belonged.

A letter from Laura Witcher poignantly tells of Uncle Silas's passing at the ranch house:

Silas seemed to pick up after I came home (from a trip) *– was more cheerful – But cough never let up and he was so very ill. He would dread the long nights. I would sit with him to a late hour and then he would say for me to go to bed – I left my door partly open and could watch the light go on and off every ten or fifteen minutes. We talked much* of friends, families and places – very little of his going. However, he told me when I came home, he tho't the beginning of the end had come – We all tho't so, as we had nothing to build any hopes on – All we could do was take care of him – Friday morning he ate a very good late breakfast – Told Mrs. Douglas not to be stingy with the oatmeal. This was his last meal. The doctor was out about noon and I had a nurse come out Friday as we saw maybe the end was near – He seemed very low Friday for awhile – I sat by his bed while he slept – When he woke up he smiled and said "I came back, didn't I." Saturday morning when I went in to see him he asked me if I was happy – I told him if he was, I was better. He says "I am – Have had the best night's rest for so long." He tried to talk much to me but I cried so and we would stop. He told me he was not afraid to die – He had nothing to fear. Talked of life as it came to him and accepted it without any bitterness and the worst had not been too bad. Spoke of friends, especially his older friends and called a number of them by name – I tried to give him a spoonful of coffee, only one swallow he took – About that time he told me he only dreaded to suffer – I said "Silas, we are not going to let you suffer anymore" – The doctor came and left the room – I heard him say to the doctor he had a million comforts and was so thankful – He continued in his right mind, talked to Paul (his brother, my grandfather, who was there with him), Mrs. Douglas, and the nurse to just a few minutes before the end – Always with a smile – So peaceful his going – You would never realized, had you not have known a death was in the house – Just went thru an open door to new realities – melted away like a snowflake on the river – A moment seen then gone forever.

Silas Pinion died Saturday, August 16, 1941 and was laid to rest under the pines in Four Mile Cemetery. Uncle Silas had told Laura that the mountains were his temples of worship. One of his favorite songs, "Home on the Range," was sung at his funeral in Cripple Creek. His peaceful death, at home where he wanted to be, occurred some forty years before I arrived with a "new" program. This was the kind of hospice experience that I hoped I could enable other people in the area to have as their lives ended.

76 Ranch, 1941

The Ponderosa Country Store and House, Lake George

CHAPTER 8

MOVING TO LAKE GEORGE

In June 1982, I moved from Denver to Lake George, a location that met the state hospice licensing requirement of being no more than 45 miles from any part of the service area. Finding housing was not easy, mainly because there were simply not many houses in Lake George. Midge Harbour, an ardent supporter of Prospect and a columnist for both the Teller and Park County newspapers, suggested that I contact Jim and Joan Spigner at the Ponderosa Country Store in Lake George. They lived above the store but also owned a rental house on the property. I introduced myself and my project and found two more willing supporters.

The little red house behind the store was being repaired following a fire, but it would be available at the end of June. Perfect. Its location on Highway 24 would enable me to get out in winter weather. It had electricity, water, a telephone, and propane for heating water and for fueling a wall heater between the two bedrooms. Such luxury! The school bus stopped in front of the store – another plus, notwithstanding the unfortunate but hardly surprising fact that Leigh Anne, a ninth grader and totally unaccustomed to rural life, was horrified at the prospect of "living in the boonies," as she christened Lake George. Indeed, ˙ this adventure was not her idea; she was happy in her junior high school in the Denver suburbs.

Relocating her for the second time in as many years could have posed major problems, but the perfect solution was waiting at Woodland Park High School. On one of my weekly trips to the area, I met with a guidance counselor at the school, explaining my dilemma and describing my daughter. I needed a ninth grade girl with whom I could connect her. He provided the ideal match in Theresa Wogaman. Her family adopted Leigh Anne as their fifth child. She kept a change of clothes at their home near the school and spent many a night there whenever weather precluded the twenty mile trip out to Lake George.

My indebtedness to Leigh Anne's second family extends far beyond "thank you." They bailed me out of many bad-weather situations and enabled Leigh Anne to participate in after-school activities. She and Theresa were best friends through high school, went to college together, and remain close. The Wogaman's stray child continues to be part of their family.

* * *

At the end of June my mother came from Virginia to help me move from Denver to Lake George. I think she had a case of insatiable curiosity – to learn first hand about the adventure I was embarking upon and where I was going to live. And, too, she wanted to see the old ranch. With furniture loaded in a U-Haul truck and my little Toyota station wagon packed to the gills, including Leigh Anne's hopelessly stressed out cat shedding hair all over the car, we drove to Lake George. Whatever negative thoughts Mom might have entertained upon arriving at my new home, she was kind enough to keep to herself. Granted, it was basically a small cabin, probably originally built for summer use, but it was definitely cute. Though I had tried to prepare her for my upcoming rural existence, its proximity to Pikes Peak, which held nothing but fond memories for her, was probably its saving grace. I could sense her excitement as we drove past that massive landmark.

My Home and Prospect's First Office

By the time the truck arrived and the furniture was unloaded and placed, the little red cabin looked enough like a home to pass muster, even though my early-marriage, eastern taste in furniture was hardly appropriate. At least the necessary pieces fit in the small space. Needless to say, this place wasn't going to be on any tour of homes. An Italian Provincial style dining table and chairs with brocade seats were poignant reminders of a drastic lifestyle change. In a fortuitous peace-keeping move, Leigh Anne's belongings, including a baby grand piano, television, and furniture that wouldn't fit anywhere else were placed in the larger of the two bedrooms. I hoped she would be pleasantly surprised when she returned from a visit with her dad in Virginia. The smaller bedroom was roomy enough for my bed (a king-size relic from my past), a chest of drawers, and one nightstand, all 1960's Italian Provincial, of course. My bedroom, on the northwest corner of the house, was lined with windows extending around the north and west sides. As I learned several months later, that was one cold room.

After Mom and I settled in, we began to explore. Her first walk into the national forest behind the house produced a bouquet of wildflowers unlike any I had ever seen. Bright red-orange Indian paintbrush, purple penstemon, wild iris, columbine in blue and white, and periwinkle-blue flax had put on their annual show. I, too, ventured up the hill to witness this beautiful summer phenomenon. Later, delving into the region's history, I saw old photographs of women in their long dresses and big hats holding huge armloads of flowers and waving from the Colorado Midland train that brought them to the area for weekend wildflower excursions in the late 1800's and into the 1900's.

To satisfy Mom's and my burgeoning curiosity, we ventured forth on a search for the old 76 Ranch. Armed with our photos and a local map, we drove south on Teller One from Florissant. The first stop was at Evergreen Station, a mountain version of a quick-stop store and gas station, which, in the 1800's, had been a stagecoach stop between the Cripple Creek Mining District and Florissant. We were directed a few miles southwest to the Fourmile area, where we matched photos to surroundings and the remains of the ranch. The original ranch house had burned prior to Mom and Dad's 1939 visit, and the bunk-house that survived the fire had subsequently become the ranch headquarters.

And there it was – the bunkhouse as it looked in the photo, except for a recent addition of a coat of bright yellow paint. Even the little outbuilding across from the house, also in one of the photos, was still standing. Box Canyon, a recessed rocky area on the ranch, gained notoriety when bank robbers chose that protected spot to hide out after stealing money from a bank in Cripple Creek. Even though this section of the ranch had been subdivided into spacious homesites, to us it was still the 76 Ranch.

On the way out, we spotted the Fourmile Grange Hall, looking exactly the same as in our photo of Dad and a ranch hand on horses in front of it. We truly felt as if we had taken a step back in time. So much was unchanged. As we headed back toward Florissant, marveling at our detective work, we stopped at the Fourmile Cemetery and found Uncle Silas's grave and those of some of the ranch workers, whose names Mom recognized. Poised under a stately, towering pine tree, Silas Pinion's head-stone conveyed his affinity for the mountains: "I will lift up mine eyes unto the hills." Psalm 121:1

CHAPTER 9

Starting To Work

After Mom had gone back to Virginia, the first item on my agenda was to create an office for Prospect Home Care and Hospice. The enclosed four-by-ten-foot front porch of the little red house was the obvious (and only) spot. Furnishings in the bare-bones office included – no, were limited to – a chair and a two-drawer file cabinet and small bookcase with a two-by-six-foot plank on top connecting the two to make a desk for my portable typewriter. Small as it was, the office was adequate until summer ended, which at that elevation happened sometime in August. Because the porch was unheated, the dining table became the office desk until the weather warmed up again. Little did I know, that would not happen until sometime in late June.

The corded telephone serving both home and office was handily located on the sill of an open pass-through between kitchen and porch. At first a four-party line served the agency. Not ideal, but private lines were rare.

And anyway, it wasn't like the phone was ringing off the hook. Sometime later the agency received a donation of an answering machine. It was a most welcome gift, as one Colorado hospice licensing requirement was to have a 24-hour answering and paging service. I squirmed in my seat at the Colorado Hospice Organization meetings when this compliance issue was discussed. Looking down at my notes to avoid eye contact with the other hospice directors, whose offices were located in towns and cities and posed no problem meeting this requirement, I remained silent. After all, Prospect was already a "polluted hospice," being a combination agency, and I didn't want to call attention to any more imperfections. With no such entity as a paging or answering service in the area, the Ponderosa Store, being one of the parties on the line, offered to take calls when I was out. As workable as that arrangement proved to be, I felt like the answering machine would move Prospect one step closer to legitimacy in the eyes of the other hospice directors.

So one morning before leaving for the day I attached the answering machine to the telephone. When I returned, the message light was blinking. I pressed the button, eagerly anticipating a caller requesting services, and was taken aback by a jumble of irate voices, all talking at once. The answering machine had activated whenever anyone on the party line received a call. My apologies were profuse. Soon after that embarrassing incident, Prospect was on the priority list for a private line.

With a functional office in place, I was ready to start caring for patients. But where were they? Convinced as I was that local residents could benefit from this service, securing referrals required ongoing effort. Marketing

Prospect to discharge planners at hospitals in Colorado Springs helped, but as with everything in a rural area, word of mouth proved to be the most effective means of acquiring patients. I gave talks about the program to any group that would invite me and publicized the agency by every means I could think of, including writing articles for the local newspapers. One benefit of belonging to the women's service club (Help U Club) in Lake George was that its meetings provided information about who was sick and who was or would be hospitalized. For someone with a planned surgery, Prospect's brochure was in their hands before entering the hospital. Meeting local people and explaining Prospect was high on my priority list, and I never hesitated to mention my connection to Laura Witcher and Silas Pinion, who were known to many old timers.

July 24, 1982
I was in the Florissant post office talking to the postmaster about Prospect and asking if he knew of any sick people. A woman in there joined in the conversation. Turned out to be the wife of the owner of the lumber mill. They had known Uncle Silas and Laura Witcher. I told her I was related, etc. She was so excited. Said I'd have to drop by (which I did).

My connections served me well. Being known as Silas Pinion's niece was a foot in a door more than once. I was not viewed as a foreigner coming into the area (from a city, no less) with a strange new program. Each such encounter solidified my presence in this territory that I was beginning to claim as my own.

August 12, 1982
   I had a most enjoyable experience on Monday. I finally
ran into this Jim Witcher I'd been looking for. I asked him
if he'd known Laura Witcher. He looked at me real funny
and said, "She's my (step)grandmother." So we proceeded
to have a conversation about my connection, etc. He took
me to lunch at the hotel in Fairplay and told me all about
the old ranching days, the family, what happened to all the
land, etc. He had nothing but the best to say about Laura
Belle and Si Pinion – How smart they both were, how she
became part of their family and was so unselfish with eve-
ryone, and how well Uncle Silas adapted to the ranching
business. He told about Laura and Si making a quarter mil-
lion dollars one year on the ranch. He had a lot of respect
for both of them. Jim is so nice – a real cowboy of the past.
Still rides his horses and wears his cowboy boots and hat.

Jim was a former mayor of Fairplay and was a good
contact to have. We met for occasional lunches. Unfortunately, advanced macular degeneration prevented his
identifying people in many of his old ranch pictures.

Frequent contacts with local physicians kept Prospect's
services in the forefront of their minds. Not having had a
home care or hospice program previously available, one
Woodland Park doctor was hesitant to refer his patients,
but eventually even he accepted the idea that this service
just might be useful. Having the doctors' cooperation was
essential because a physician's order was required before
care could be provided. The American Medical Association
insisted on the physician's order requirement as a condition of approval of the home care benefit package when
Medicare was enacted. Doctors wanted control.

Even though a home care nurse evaluates a patient and writes a care plan, it and subsequent renewals must have the physician's signature, necessitating visits to doctors' offices or, in the days before facsimile machines, communicating by U.S. mail with physicians in Colorado Springs or Denver. A copy of the signed order had to be mailed with a bill for services or the charge would be denied by Medicare.

Though every referral did not add a hospice or home care patient to the caseload, I didn't say no to anything. I removed sutures and was given a monetary donation. I supervised an alcoholic's ingestion of Antabuse, and he supplied me with venison. I did a lot of counseling and advising. I gave allergy shots in exchange for firewood. Many contacts offered payment in the form of food, which was fine with me.

August 12, 1982
Today I got paid with a walker, ten cans of Ensure, and four pieces of fudge.

Aside from a desire to help local people, I perceived my small acts of kindness as a marketing bonus, possibly generating an eventual referral or a request for services. As is often the case in rural areas, the country store served as a local communications hub. While privacy was respected, local residents knew each other and were concerned about neighbors' problems. Sharing information fell under the umbrella of helping and caring for and about others. Joan at the Ponderosa Store often connected me to potential patients, always in a most discreet manner, and later on, to nursing staff.

One of Prospect's first referrals came from the public health nurse in Fairplay. The patient was a young gunshot victim from an argument that he had lost. He lived in the old mining town of Alma at 10,361 feet elevation. The young man resided in a 100-year-old miner's cabin precariously perched on the side of a steep slope. My first clue about Alma was revealed when I walked in the door and saw down-filled coats hanging on pegs by the front door. It was August. In Alma, winter clothes were never put away. The cramped cabin was home to several happy young people who nonchalantly passed a marijuana cigarette from one to the next, including the patient, who was drinking beer and desperately trying to absent himself from the pain that I was about to inflict.

His answers to questions about his pain medication suggested that he had obtained different narcotics from several physicians in surrounding towns as well as the emergency room in Fairplay. I tried not to act horrified at the thought, especially since he had probably taken several potent drugs at one time prior to my arrival. In my former life as a health department employee, I would have thought about legal implications. Common sense prevailed, however, and I knew that keeping the entry-exit bullet wound that tunneled through his upper arm free from infection had to be my focus.

So I set to work trying to establish a sterile field in this setting with no running water and hundreds of flies. The only available work space was a low table around which his audience of observing friends was seated. I opened the dressing-change pack and donned sterile gloves. Using the forceps in the pack I pulled a couple of feet of antibiotic impregnated gauze from the wound as the patient cringed and his compatriots moaned and gagged. After the bullet's passageway was irrigated with sterile saline, the wound re-packed with new gauze, and a clean dressing applied, the crowd cheered and continued passing the joint around. As casual as they were about it, I was expecting them to offer it to me. The patient tolerated the dressing changes and wound packing with the resources available to him – narcotics, beer and marijuana. I was the only person of serious demeanor in the room.

After several more visits and dressing changes the wound had closed with no sign of infection. I didn't mind that there was no source of payment. I was pleased that the outcome had been successful, that the public health nurse had referred a patient, and also that she had made arrangements for the hospital to provide all of the supplies that I needed. This casual small-town way of getting things accomplished was a definite plus.

CHAPTER 10

WELCOME GIFTS

Generous donations helped keep Prospect afloat in that first struggling year – free photocopying at a bank in Woodland Park and the hospital in Fairplay, the Ponderosa Store as the initial answering service, medical supplies from physicians and hospitals, reduced charges for towing and repairs from Gilley's Lake George garage, and welcome contributions of food (including game that I had to learn how to cook) and firewood. As a former government employee, I was not used to accepting gifts, but this was a different situation entirely. Appreciative people wanted and needed to say "thank you." Others wanted to show support for a program that was looking like it might be important to the community.

Jim and Joan at the Ponderosa Store helped stretch my food budget by giving me produce that, though too ripe to sell, was fine by my standards, bread that was past the sell-by date, and anything else they thought I could use. Jim was instrumental in arranging for Prospect's private phone line. He gave me scrap lumber to burn and cut dead trees to add to my firewood supply. Indeed, the Spigners were key to my survival.

July 9, 1982
Today the Spigners gave me a bag of popcorn, eight grapefruit, two dozen oranges, three tomatoes and a head of lettuce. I'm going to like that store.

My aunt, who believed that I was out in the mountains doing missionary work, sent three huge boxes of home care equipment and supplies gathered from members of her church in Tennessee. Letters of encouragement came with monetary contributions from friends back east, and I began to realize that many people were solidly behind this effort with their hopes and prayers as well as their checkbooks.

During the first year I paid myself only mileage reimbursement, which amounted to as much as $500 per month, usually enough to scrape by on, out of Medicare checks and contributions from my family and others. Frugality was always part of my nature, so lack of money didn't cause too many overt changes in my lifestyle. The major impact was mental, seeing my savings evaporate and the checking account dwindle to nothing each month. I knew that Leigh Anne and I had everything we really needed and that our lives were rich in aspects other than financial. We had a roof over our heads, food to eat, an automobile that usually functioned well, and supportive and caring friends and family. I had faith that somehow we would be taken care of, and we were.

August 12, 1982

It's easy to forget my problems when I visit people who have real problems. And I feel very lucky to be in this beautiful part of the country, to have a nice place to live, and to have family who love me. Thank you for that.

I resorted to such cost-cutting measures as buying packages of 24 chicken backs (four meals' worth) for a dollar, a special at the grocery store in Woodland Park. As long as they were fried, Leigh Anne thought they were great. Unfortunately, she wasn't fond of most other low-budget meals I produced. At one point she asked why we were having beans so often. I could always sell her on an omelet, pancakes, or French toast. Thank goodness for the resiliency of the human body, as we most certainly weren't into health food that year.

My attempts at cutting my own hair were producing dire results.

August 20, 1982

I decided that the time had come when I could no longer put off getting a haircut. So I went in to the hair place this morning and told the girl why my hair was so chopped up and what my situation was (starting home care and hospice program with no money) but that I decided ten dollars for a haircut would be a good investment for me right now. When she finished, I thanked her and said it was ten dollars well spent. And she said, "No, this one's on me. You've been out there helping everyone else, and it sounds like it's time someone did something for you." I hugged her.

My parents and sisters offered the encouragement I needed to survive during the early months. As independent and self-sufficient as I had always been, accepting the realization that I needed financial help was no small pill to swallow. I felt like a failure when I reached the point of asking my parents for a loan.

August 26, 1982
Just a quick note to let you know that the check ($1,000) was in the mailbox when I got home last night. I can never thank you enough. I feel like a huge weight is off my shoulders today. I bought some groceries and school supplies for Leigh Anne, typing paper, and light bulbs. Tonight I'm going through the bills and will decide how little I can get by with paying on each one.

An original plan for supplemental funding failed to materialize and was a definite setback. In addition to that lack of anticipated income, a glitch in Medicare's payment process delayed Prospect's reimbursements for the first two months of Medicare home care claims. After a red-tape error was corrected, Medicare payments arrived as expected and the cash flow improved.

CHAPTER 11

INITIAL STAFF

In the early days, Prospect had only a skeleton staff – the disciplines required to meet federal and state home care and hospice certification requirements (nurse, therapists, home health aide, and social worker). They were paid per visit from Medicare reimbursement for services. Initially, I was the only nurse, and also served as home health aide in the outlying areas. A home health aide in Woodland Park provided personal care visits in the eastern end of the service area. The existence of all the required workers in our remote area was an unexpected bonus. They were people who lived in the mountains and wanted to work in the mountains.

In a 1982 economy that forced many onto the job-less rolls, survival was a challenge, especially in an area where jobs were hard to find in the best of times. These were eager workers, excited to learn that they would be able to use their skills in our area. Prospect's staff realized that such a sparsely populated area would not provide a sufficient volume of hospice and home care patients to support them, even in a lifestyle of basic necessities. They agreed that in spite of altruistic motivation, reality dictated that they would need additional means of ensuring personal survival.

The social worker worked several evenings a week as a cook and bartender, taught a cooking class, wrote a weekly newspaper column, played piano in a neighboring town's nightspot, and cleaned condominiums in a ski area – all so that she could live in the mountains. The occupational therapist started a business making insulated window shades. One nurse, who was hired later, spent every weekend working four straight shifts in a hospital 150 miles away to earn enough to support herself and her son in their mountain lifestyle for the remainder of the week. These people were resourceful, a definite plus for Prospect. My respect for each one grew as their talents, skills and abilities became apparent along with their determination to survive in the mountains.

Nurses and aides were selected based on experience, skill and comfort in home care situations. The ability to show compassion was a must. It takes a certain personality – confident, assertive, and maybe a bit gutsy – to go into homes of strangers and establish an immediate connection. First impressions do count. Alone in a home, a nurse or aide has no supervisor or head nurse to consult. Many homes in the area had no telephone, so summoning assistance or a second opinion was out of the question. Prospect's nurses and aides had to be confident of their skills and independent judgment and at the same time mindful of limitations and restrictions. One nurse, who inquired about a position, wanted to do hospice and home care work but had never done either. I explained our need for experienced staff. Several months later she called to say that she had completed a hospice training course and was working part time for a home care agency. Her persistence and resolution of deficiencies paid off. Sometime later she joined Prospect's staff.

Home health aides are the unsung heroes of home care. They are providers of personal care – bathing and toileting, cleaning the patient environment, and occasionally preparing a meal. Two of Prospect's aides had partially completed nursing school – a bonus in our situation. All staff needed to be able to assist a patient to the bathroom or on and off of a bedpan, do a bed bath, prepare something to eat, and feed a bedbound patient if the need arose. Interestingly, most of Prospect's nurses and therapists were not only willing to do personal care but had worked as aides previously. And all were willing to participate in hospice training and inservice education. Another bonus.

Physical, occupational, and speech therapists are the major providers of home care when a patient needs to be rehabilitated from a stroke or any condition that results in weakness or impairment. Implementing such a program in some of our patients' homes was an interesting challenge. Quarters too small to accommodate a wheelchair or walker, narrow doorways, tiny bathrooms – or a bedside commode crammed into a bedroom – all made their work difficult but not impossible. Much to their credit, they helped many people regain an acceptable level of functioning in spite of a far from ideal work environment. For home care therapists as well as nurses, successfully carrying out procedures in inhospitable settings, with sometimes improvised or adapted equipment, produces an incomparable sense of accomplishment, especially when patients are able to progress to a desired goal.

Early in my groundwork days I met an occupational therapist in Fairplay who had tried to generate interest in a home care agency to serve that area. She was an avid supporter of Prospect and became one of the first staff members. Occupational therapy helps people adapt to functional limitations caused by disease or injury, sometimes making structural changes to a home, such as removing doors or building wheelchair ramps, and often using ingenious assistive devices to promote patient independence.

One day she and I visited a wheelchair-bound paraplegic man who lived in a trailer house in Jefferson. She had obtained a sliding shower seat that we hoped would enable him to take a shower without assistance. He would have to transfer from his wheelchair onto the seat and then slide the seat into the shower stall. We needed to see if he could use this piece of equipment in his cramped bathroom. I was there to help with the shower if necessary. Somehow in his attempt to transfer onto the seat, the naked patient ended up on the bathroom floor. His ample girth and excess padding not only softened his landing but also posed a problem getting him off the floor. For a minute or so all three of us were laughing too hard to do anything. Then I watched in awe as this petite therapist squatted down, anchored herself behind him, her back braced against the wall, and with her skinny little arms under his, raised this heavy guy up onto the shower seat. Her knowledge and skill in executing body mechanics saved the day.

Prospect's volunteers supplemented the services that professional staff offered to hospice and home care families. Although volunteers were typically part of a hospice team, we offered volunteer services to home care families as well, to visit with a patient while the caregiver took a break or ran errands. Caring for a dying person at home usually requires many hours of hospice support, not only for the patient but especially for family members. Along with an increasing caregiving burden, they are dealing with their own emotions, seeing a loved one decline physically and anticipating the time when death will come. A trained volunteer can help a family accomplish its mission successfully by being an understanding listener and attending to a variety of needs. Continued counseling by a bereavement volunteer after a patient death guides a family through the process of grieving their loss and facing the future.

Prospect needed a person to train and supervise its volunteers. I met that person at a party. We were discussing an article that I had written for the local newspaper, and she expressed an interest in doing hospice work. She was a volunteer counselor at the mental health center and was taking a course on working with the terminally ill and their families. Having dealt with significant losses in her own life, she believed that she had a contribution to make. She was the ideal person to establish a volunteer program and develop a bereavement service.

Other volunteers followed – a massage therapist who offered to help with pain management problems, a music therapist who would take her portable piano to the home of any patient who would enjoy hearing favorite songs or hymns. I never imagined having these unique services that many large hospices could only wish for.

CHAPTER 12

SUMMER STORM

I n 1982 few roads, especially in the western section of the service area, were paved. U.S. Highway 24 spanned the area from east to west. The other paved roads were Teller County 67, north out of Woodland Park and south from Divide to Cripple Creek and Victor; Park County 9 from Hartsel northwest to Fairplay and Alma, and south to Guffey; and U.S. Highway 285 from Denver through Jefferson, Fairplay and on south.

But patients didn't live on these main roads. Back roads, usually in marginal condition, provided the only access to most homes, some of which were quite isolated. To familiarize myself with the area, I took many Sunday drives, exploring roads and parts of the country that were new to me. Along the way were old cabins that spoke of the area's history. My imagination pictured early settlers eking out a bare-bones existence, and I especially thought of the women and children, facing hardships on a daily basis. Those who survived must have been incredibly tough.

Early Home, Lake George Area

Survival was on my mind one sunny day in the late summer of 1982 when I ventured into unknown (to me) territory to find a new patient who had been referred by another patient. Obtaining referrals was one challenge, but finding homes in the more remote areas was another issue entirely. I suspected from the description of this new patient's location that I was headed into the middle of nowhere. The directions included landmarks such as "hill," "curve," "old cabin," "fence." After leaving the first patient's house in mid-afternoon, I began following the directions he provided. Fourteen miles down a dirt washboard I turned as directed, though there were no residences in sight.

By this time, afternoon thunderstorms were building in the west. The sky darkened, and lightning and thunder began. A desolate dirt road led me up and down hills and around curves for about ten minutes. Not having seen a sign of life or even so much as a cabin since making the last turn, I realized that I was heading for nothing but more desolation. Then came the rain – a deluge the likes of which I had never seen. Visibility: Zero. Wind: Furious. Water: Everywhere. And there I was, at the bottom of a steep hill, sitting at the road's end. Torrents of muddy water poured toward me, carving deep gullies out of this poor excuse for a road. Lightning flashed and thunder cracked. I prayed and prayed some more. *"Please,* God, if you can hear me above this racket, get me out of this mess." I hoped I wouldn't be stuck there forever. Since this was an unplanned visit, no one (including me) knew where I was. How would anyone even look for me?

"God," I said again in a most serious voice, "if you want me out here doing this work, I certainly can't stay here." My only choice of escaping was to attempt to drive up this road that had deteriorated before my eyes. Holding my breath and clutching the steering wheel, I bumped and swerved my way up the hill through the slime, guided by the ruts in the road. As miracles go, I indeed escaped, but by this time, hail was pounding on the car in a deafening roar. I started to laugh (what else?). I couldn't believe I was being subjected to such a rude initiation to mountain weather. Hoping to get back to the place where I had turned, I forged ahead despite not being able to see more than five feet in front of the car. I certainly didn't have to worry about meeting another vehicle. No idiot would have been out in that mess. Trying to stay on the road was the challenge of the moment.

I vaguely remembered having seen a derelict mobile home off in the trees not far from the previous turn-off. I spotted it again and cautiously turned in on what looked like a driveway. An old pickup truck was parked in front, so there was a chance that the place was occupied. I pulled into the yard and armed with an umbrella that , turned inside out the moment that I raised it, ran to the door through the mud, hoping that my knocking might be heard over the hailstones pummeling the metal structure. To my great joy and downright amazement, someone opened the door to a stranger in less than ideal visiting conditions.

Considering the range of possibilities as to what could have been inside the trailer, I was thankful to find a father, mother, and two little girls all huddled in the dark, waiting for the fury to abate. I wasted no time explaining who I was and how I happened to be in that spot at that moment. They knew the place I was trying to find and told me how to get there. As I thought about how I could have made so many wrong turns, it became apparent that the patient who had given the directions had his rights and lefts reversed. I sat through the worst of the storm with these friendly folks and then headed on my way, feeling a surge of confidence (or was it amazement?) for keeping my cool on the first of numerous confrontations with Mother Nature. An angel was definitely on my shoulder during that adventure.

CHAPTER 13

AUTUMN GOLD

When the temperature began to drop in September, Jim Spigner installed a much needed wood stove in the living room. As I wrote to my parents, keeping warm was beginning to present a challenge.

September 8, 1982

Winter is coming. There was a little snow on Pikes Peak earlier this week. Jim says he is starting to work on installing the wood stove this weekend. It's about 56 degrees in here in the mornings, but it doesn't seem that cold. I sleep under ten pounds of blankets and still have frozen feet, even with fuzzy socks on. It gets warm during the day and is really nice – until the afternoon thunderstorms come through. I never know what to wear. I'm trying to spend a couple of hours every weekend collecting dead wood up behind the house. I'm sure it will burn like paper, but it will help. Hate to buy wood. Don't know which is more expensive – wood or propane. Jim told me last week I have 55 gallons left of my first

100 gallons. I'm sure if I started heating with it, it would go fast.

If Leigh Anne didn't have a school activity on a Saturday, she and I would go up into the National Forest behind the house to get firewood. There was plenty of it lying on the ground. I took my hatchet and chopped it into usable lengths. Then we loaded it onto an old sheet and dragged it down the hill to our wood pile. The dead wood did burn quickly, but it was good for getting a fire started.

September lived up to its reputation of being spectacular, with quaking aspens turning bright gold and the mountains donning their white winter coats. The open space and blue sky framing the aspens created an environment of sheer beauty year after year. In a September 19, 1938 letter Uncle Silas wrote,

"We are having real autumn weather – the sky so blue and clear. It looks as if one could almost reach up and touch it."

And forty-four years later, that's exactly how it looked to me.

Work days were long and consisted of a lot of driving, usually about 100 to 150 miles. My car was loaded with supplies and equipment – whatever I needed for the day's visits plus any donated equipment I thought might be useful to a patient or family. I always carried plenty of food and water, never sure how long I might be out. I kept a sleeping bag and warm clothing in the back, in the event that I might have car trouble or somehow be stranded overnight.

I tried to plan visits and contacts so that I would travel in some kind of an efficient pattern – Jefferson, Fairplay, Alma on one day; Green Mountain Falls, Woodland Park, Cripple Creek, Victor on another. Nevertheless, there were occasional 300 mile days when a procedure had to be done at a certain time at each end of the area on the same day and sometimes twice a day.

September 22, 1982
Did I tell you that I got two new patients last week? One has been in the hospital this week but will be out tomorrow. The other I got last Saturday when one of the doctors called and asked if I could come in "right now" and make a home visit with him. So of course I did. And then I visited again at 11:30 Saturday night and 7:30 Sunday morning and have visited at 7:00 every day this week. He has to have blood drawn every morning. Then I have to take the blood to Colorado Springs to the lab. Needless to say, I've gotten a lot of business done in the Springs this week. Have also driven a lot. One day I went from home to Woodland Park to Colorado Springs to Fairplay and Alma to home and in to Woodland Park again. Yikes! I think that tomorrow and Fri. may look like that. Pray that the car stays healthy.

I became adept at my version of "meals on wheels" – lunch while driving. Peeling an orange was an accomplishment. The saving grace of all those hours behind the wheel was the spectacular scenery. Distant snowcapped peaks to the south, west, and north framed the vast expanse of South Park. Red tail hawks and golden eagles soared above, and a beautiful bald eagle often circled the South Platte River on the western edge of Lake George. Deer, antelope, and elk were frequent sights in this wide-open country, as were cattle and horses, grazing on the range. I smiled as I drove, thankful to be carving out an existence and a means of doing work that I loved in such awesome surroundings.

Back Road Traffic

Communication in the days before cellular telephones and, in fact, before telephone service was widely available in this rural area, proved to be an obstacle to be reckoned with.

September 27, 1982
The most sparsely populated part of the area has several hundred people living out there with a total of four phones. Those four people serve as contacts for everyone else. They use CB radios when they can transmit a signal – or the mail, but that means going to the post office, which is about 30

miles away for some of them. There are chronically ill, elderly people living alone in these isolated areas. But it's what they're used to. They wouldn't have it any other way. In the more rural, western end of the service area I don't have a single staff member who has a phone. Many of these places just can't get phone service yet.

U.S. Mail was my means of communication with staff unless I happened to find someone at home on a trip to her area. The eastern end of the service area, being relatively close to Colorado Springs, had telephones in all but the outlying parts. If I needed to call a patient or staff member while I was out, I used a pay phone or a telephone in a patient's home. So the real problem was in the vast South Park area.

I frequently visited a couple who lived in the most remote and isolated part of Prospect's service area. To reach their home I drove west from Lake George, over Wilkerson Pass, across South Park, and then north on the unpaved Elkhorn Road for about 15 miles before turning into an area dotted with an occasional cabin or trailer house. On several winter visits my cross-country skis were in the car, and I never ventured out there without telling the Ponderosa Store where I was going.

Alan and Joann, both of whom were chronic lung disease patients on oxygen, insisted that they felt better where they lived at 10,000 feet than down in air-polluted Denver at half the altitude. The brown ceiling of their trailer house and the telltale odor of cigarette smoke, fresh and stale, painted a picture of many years of heavy smoking. I never saw Alan and Joann without a lighted cigarette in hand, seated in their chairs, short of breath, with oxygen tubing tangled on the floor between them. My hope was that the place would not go up in flames, at least not while I was there. If they chose to meet their demise in an inferno, so be it, but it wasn't what I wanted. Alan's dose of steroids and other medication for his lung disease had to be adjusted frequently due to the instability of his condition. Because there was no telephone service in that area, I normally phoned his Denver pulmonologist after returning home from a visit to report Alan's condition. The physician would then make any necessary changes in medication orders, which I would implement on my next visit. On one occasion I detected serious medication side effects and needed to communicate with Alan's doctor immediately. The solution in this situation was for Alan to call on his citizen's band (CB) radio to a friend in Jefferson and have that man relay the information to the doctor by phone. More than a little concerned that the message might not be transmitted accurately, I knew we had no choice but to try. I overheard via the CB what the friend was telling the doctor by phone, and it was correct (whew). The next challenge was for the doctor's reply, being relayed one sentence at a time via the friend on his CB radio, to be the medication change that was intended. The new dose as communicated seemed appropriate, so I made the change. When I arrived home I called the physician to confirm the order. He and I had a good laugh over that unusual sample of rural home care.

CHAPTER 14

Support And Encouragement

September brought Prospect its first actual hospice patient. Prospect had several home care patients by then, but this lady was the first to receive hospice care. At that point, I functioned as her nurse, home health aide and volunteer. In reality her care was all voluntary, as she had no source of payment. She was not yet Medicare age, and her private insurance, like most at the time, did not cover hospice care. Fortunately, she lived only a few miles from me, so travel time and mileage were not issues. I was happy using my skills for anyone who needed the service. Payment would have been welcome, but it was not my priority. Even though this lady did not die at home – she spent her last few days in a hospital – her husband became one of Prospect's staunch supporters. After her death, contributions in her memory poured in. Her appreciative husband stated adamantly that this service was needed in the community and he intended for Prospect "to make it." He provided firewood, my October rent payment, transportation when my car was being repaired, and plenty of encouragement.

September 29, 1982
I appreciate so much what everyone is doing to help me. I still have some moments of thinking that I might not survive, but I probably should keep at it for the people who might benefit from the service. I think it's important for me to keep trying. One day at a time. I have lots of people here offering support and encouragement. The husband of the lady who died just called, and he has another check for me that came in his mail. And he is having a cord of wood delivered to me next week. He says he wants to keep me going. Amazing.

* * *

In spite of the beauty of fall, the early snows proved to be a challenge. I never had another snow adventure to match that of the season's first big storm, October 7, 1982, a day indelibly etched in my memory. My plan for the day was to go into Woodland Park and watch my cheerleader daughter in the homecoming parade in the morning and then to go down to Colorado Springs to buy snow tires. The flakes started falling at 7:00 a.m. By 9:30 a.m. I had decided to skip the parade and head straight for Colorado Springs. As is characteristic of fall and spring snows, the roads became slick rapidly - too slick for a lightweight two-wheel-drive vehicle without snow tires and carrying only about three gallons of gas in the tank. At only five miles per hour my car would start sliding. The wheels spun on the slightest incline. I just wanted to go back home. Fortunately traffic was scarce, as I was all over the road in Florissant Canyon, with no place to turn around. More than a little frightened, with the canyon being a succession of curves and drop-offs, I envisioned someone rounding a curve, only to find my car facing them on the wrong side of the two-lane road. My worries were momentarily relieved when I slid into a ditch and came to a stop facing the direction from which I had come. Oh, boy – headed home. Somehow, after a couple of tries, I drove out of the ditch and back onto the road, but much to my chagrin, a 180 degree spin sent me heading east once again and unable to negotiate the slight hill in front of me.

The highway was getting slicker by the minute, and soon, even two miles per hour sent me sideways. At that point I was rescued by none other than the husband of the first hospice patient, who had died two weeks before. While I maneuvered the car back into the proper lane, Don halted a large delivery truck as it rounded the curve behind me. Without another moment's hesitation, I steered my car off the road, plowed headlong into the nearest snow bank, and abandoned the useless vehicle without a second thought. I heard later that the highway had been closed due to the number of accidents and slides off the road.

Luckily for me, Don was on his way to Colorado Springs to buy snow tires. I piled into his heavy truck and we inched ahead. He insisted on buying my studded snow tires and then delivering me to Gilley's Lake George garage. Bob and Tom retrieved my car with their tow truck. Jimmy at the gas station mounted the new tires and had me back in business several hours later. I learned that he had refused everyone else that day because of the horrible weather. Not only was an angel on my shoulder in that storm, local folks stepped up to look out for me. They were angels, too. I was learning an important lesson: As I gave of my time and skills, the community gave back to me in countless ways. Again and again I was taken care of.

November 21, 1982
I'm getting more frequent calls as "the neighborhood nurse." Yesterday I got a call from a young mother of a 4-year-old, a 20-month-old and a 5-month-old. Everyone had a stomach virus and she was worried about the babies getting dehydrated. My other call was to go see a little old lady who had fallen a week ago and had cut her head and hand, is Christian Scientist and won't go to a doctor. I'll probably see her a few more times. She asked how much the visit cost and of course, I said, "Nothing." She lives in a little old motel cabin and obviously doesn't have much money. Oh, well.

There were "up" times and there were "down" times that first year. On days when my faith wavered and I let worries consume me, I was certain that this venture represented an absolute loss of mental faculties, let alone common sense. Realizing that the agency was not yet providing me with a living wage, I had momentary lapses wishing for my more than adequate salary from my health department days in Virginia. In November and December of 1982 the patient census was low, and referrals few and far between. I sometimes wondered if this home care and hospice idea would ever catch on. Yet whenever negative thoughts prevailed, something would happen to get me back on track.

December 14, 1982
In today's mail was a $1,000 contribution from a couple I've never met. I don't even know how they heard about me. It was in a Christmas card, and it said, "We are avid supporters of the hospice movement. Hope the enclosed will be of some aid in the furtherance of your dedication to your community and hospice goals." What a wonderful surprise! (This couple, from elsewhere in the state, gave the same donation the following Christmas.)

Why did I ever doubt?

CHAPTER 15

WINTER WONDERLAND

That first year in the mountains provided a crash course in contending with the weather. The winter of 1982-83 produced more snow than the old timers vowed they had ever seen. And it was cold. Snow piled up from the infamous Christmas Eve blizzard until May. Words like "ground blizzard," "whiteout," and "black ice" became part of my vocabulary. The dry snow in the west blew and drifted, unlike the wet snow that I had experienced in the east. The ground could be almost bare in one spot and nearby the snow would be several feet deep where the wind had blown it. Highway 285 between Jefferson and Fairplay was known for having severe whiteouts, blizzard conditions with zero visibility resulting in frequent accidents. I would drive back roads to avoid that stretch of highway. In spite of the assortment of problems caused by a heavy snowstorm, I loved the beauty created by a blanket of fresh snow against the clarity of a deep blue sky. And I loved the silence of snow, when the only sound was an occasional snow plop falling from a pine tree. The sight of a herd of deer or elk foraging in the snow was reason enough to stop along the road.

December 31, 1982

Last day of 1982 – also the coldest so far. My thermometer says minus 20 degrees and mine is usually 8 to 10 degrees higher than the actual temperature. I imagine it is close to minus 30. It is 48 degrees in my bedroom. The gas heater is set at 55, and it has been on ever since the fire burned out at some point in the night. There is ice on the inside of the windows. We had frozen pipes again yesterday morning. Jim got them thawed out and insulated yesterday, so, thank goodness, we do have water today. This weather sure eats up the firewood. My office is not much warmer than the outdoors. The apples I stored out there froze, so I made applesauce last night. Now I use the office for drying out firewood that has been out in the snow.

I have a new patient -- an 80 year old lady who had a stroke three weeks ago. She and her husband live on a ranch that is owned by her daughter and son-in-law. It's a church camp or something. Anyway, it's about four miles north of Woodland Park up Rampart Range Road. I'm to call when I'm leaving Woodland Park, drive till I get stuck, and then they'll come after me in a four-wheel-drive vehicle. The man sounded really nice and said they have lots of help around to dig me out of the snow. Sounds like an interesting adventure.

January 2, 1983

I made it to all three of my visits on Friday. Slid a lot getting back into that ranch, but they didn't have to dig me out.

A bunch of boys were shoveling for me when I got there. It is about five miles from Woodland Park. It is beautiful up there. Up real high. Good views. I'm surprised the car made it.

Winter weather was challenge enough, but occasional car trouble or a flat tire was an added inconvenience. Those untimely events were inevitable with all of the miles I was driving and the condition of the roads. Whenever I had a problem, someone always came to my rescue. I was absolutely sure that an angel was on my shoulder.

January 21, 1983

Had a flat tire out near Hartsel on Wednesday. I had just gotten on the highway, from a visit 15 miles up the Elkhorn Road. I didn't see another human being the whole way in or out. The road was so bad I didn't realize the tire was flat till I got to the highway. Had to flag down a guy because I couldn't get the nuts undone, even jumping on the lug wrench. It was one of the snow tires they had put on at the tire place. I had to drive the rest of the way on one studded snow tire and one bald spare and the roads were a snowy mess. Then yesterday I had to go to Colorado Springs to get the tire replaced. Didn't fit into my schedule at all, but more snow was coming, so I didn't dare wait. Ended up driving 230 miles yesterday and still had to cancel one visit and a meeting.

You'll be happy to know that I just got health insurance (hospitalization with a $500 deductible, nothing for accidents). I paid $43.20 extra for the accident rider for a year. The other part is $112 per quarter. Not too bad, I guess.

February 1, 1983
I think I may have to get a new starter. It is making a
funny noise. What next!
Thanks again for money, stamps, etc. Leigh Anne and I
will get haircuts this week, so that's where the $20 will go. I
paid myself $663 yesterday – to cover my travel, expenses, a
half cord of wood, and rent. Then I paid all my bills. I should
have enough to get through the month. I'm burning a lot of
wood but it sure is nice to be warm in here.

One bright winter day I had promised to take Leigh Anne skiing. I had been out the night before for a patient death and was functioning on two hours of sleep. Not wanting to disappoint Leigh Anne, I struggled out of bed and we headed toward the mountains. Near the top of Wilkerson Pass the car conked out. After several futile attempts to start it, we got out, crossed the highway, and within minutes were picked up by a nice man who delivered us to Gilley's garage in Lake George. Bob and Tom were my frequent rescuers and car fixers. They towed the car to the shop, repaired it, and got it going again, but sadly for Leigh Anne the ski day had to be postponed. I went home and slept. I hated missing an opportunity to spend a day with her, as my busy life tipped the scales to the side of child neglect. Fortunately, she and I both survived.

Days were long and visits were sometimes made at odd hours. Meetings in Denver took an inordinate amount of time, given the three-hour drive each way. Visiting a patient on the way home added hours to an already long day. Given that patient records and administrative paperwork were relegated to the evening hours, often after midnight, sleep deprivation became a habit.

Not having the time or interest for anything resembling a social life, I did carve out a few hours to attend community dances at the Four Mile Grange Hall and the old Florissant school house. These events had a long history in the area and probably bore a striking resemblance to the dances of 100 years earlier. Local musicians sang old songs and played fiddles, guitars, and mandolins. People of all ages came, kids included. The worn wooden floors had supported generations of dancing feet. I loved this piece of mountain fun and a chance to dance with some of the old timers.

February 4, 1983, midnight
I went to the Grange chili supper and dance tonight and just got home, so I'm not sleepy yet. It's zero degrees outside. I couldn't believe people were really going to the outhouse. The two guys I danced with were both about 75 years old. One was a wild dancer. I think he was about to have a heart attack when he left. I'm getting to know a lot of people now. They are all very nice to me.

February 8, 1983
Another long day. Gone from 8:30 a.m. till 10:30 p.m. Went to Cripple Creek twice and Woodland Park and Green Mountain Falls in between. Got a new hospice patient in Cripple Creek.

February 19, 1983
After I got back from Denver late Thursday afternoon, I made a visit to the new hospice patient in Cripple Creek.

Picked up Leigh Anne in Woodland Park about 7:30 p.m. Got home about 8:00. Got a call about a lady in Woodland Park who was in bad shape but didn't want to go to the hospital. Had to go back to Woodland Park at 9:00 p.m. to see her and got home at 4:30 a.m. She had heart failure. Finally convinced her to go to the hospital and then I went with her. Emergency rooms are very slow. I stayed till she was admitted and in a room. Got up at 7:30 Friday morning and took Leigh Anne skiing. Didn't want to disappoint her again. I'm still tired, but I'll recover. I'm trying to get caught up on paperwork this weekend. I think I'm a little too busy right now. Feast or famine.

Being on call meant occasional nighttime visits. Fortunately, Leigh Anne was old enough to be home alone and to get ready for school and out the door in time to catch the school bus. I never worried for her safety or mine. Late at night, my car was usually the only one on the road, especially in snowy weather, and my angel was always looking out for me. There was something about being out at night that I enjoyed. It was quiet and peaceful. At our altitude the stars seemed close enough to reach up and grab a handful.

Aside from minor issues, the house in Lake George proved to be about the best in the area. Compared to those of many people, our accommodations were nothing to complain about, and the Spigners watched over me like doting parents or, in my case, angels. Jim was there to help with problems like frozen pipes, and I could take care of the small stuff.

The burn smell from the house fire never quite disappeared. After much searching and sniffing I zeroed in on the offending source – the wall behind the bathroom medicine cabinet. I unloaded it, unscrewed it, took it out, and scrubbed the blackened wall. Problem solved. At one point in winter I began hearing a scratching sound during the night. Determined to find the offensive critter, I finally met it face to face one dark night. My flashlight illuminated the beady eyes of a kangaroo rat, happily and safely ensconced behind a grate covering a duct in the defunct heating system. The poor little guy (really cute) was trapped and removed. Nights were peaceful once again.

A clothes dryer occupied an unheated storage space underneath the house. By February I had scraped together enough money to by a used washer. At the completion of a wash, the hoses had to be disconnected and drained to prevent their freezing and breaking – a small price to pay for the luxury of having the appliances and avoiding the twenty-mile trip to the laundromat in Woodland Park.

Mountain living did have a downside. Our cats met their demise at the talons of owls and claws of other unknown predators. It was a sad experience indeed, especially for Leigh Anne, who had inherited my sister's cat Geraldine in Virginia, moved her to Denver and on to Lake George, only to have her carried off, screeching, one cold night. Later another cat took up residence on our back porch and used it as a birthing center. She was a beautiful creature and a wonderful mother to her litter. Leigh Anne and I really liked that cat. In another sad moment of mountain living, something bit off one of her legs one night and we had to have her euthanized. More tears. Of course everything has to eat, but we wished the menu hadn't offered our kitties. We kept two of the kittens, and the other survivors were adopted.

The Ashley stove didn't hold enough firewood to last through the night in this uninsulated cabin when the temperature dropped to minus 20 degrees. The "up" side was the incentive that a cold house provided to get out in the mornings, especially when the pipes were frozen and there was no water. The woodshed behind the house was inaccessible in winter because of deep snow and no back door. Therefore, the woodpile was just that – a pile of wood lying on the ground in front of the house where the delivery truck dumped it. In mid-winter I began rationing wood, concerned at the alarming rate of pile decline.

One day, with the wood supply running low and the propane tank nearly empty, an unusually high electric bill arrived. Leigh Anne used a hair dryer and two different curling irons every morning and insisted on turning up the propane-guzzling wall heater in her bedroom. I ranted about her energy waste and not so kindly suggested that she wear more clothes and turn down the heater. Not what she wanted to hear. As frustrated as I was, expecting her to dive wholeheartedly into this lifestyle change that I had forced on her was, I suppose, unreasonable. In the mornings the indoor temperature was usually around 40 degrees. To save firewood I didn't start a fire. The school bus came early, and I tried to be out by 8:30. In spite of a good car heater, there were mornings when my toes didn't thaw out for three hours.

March 1, 1983
  Got to head to Cripple Creek. Can't wait to get in the car and turn on the heater. Have to go to the bathroom but can't make myself sit on that cold toilet seat.

As much as I tried to convince myself that poverty was only a state of mind, my checkbook told the truth. One small comfort was that the 1982 economy had left many people without incomes and that I had plenty of company. I even rationalized that a poverty experience was character building and that I would understand more fully the plight of the indigent, having traveled that road myself. (I still believe that to be true.) Pangs of guilt surfaced as I cut Leigh Anne's allowance in half, not wanting to deprive her of things she needed just because I had embarked on a mid-life adventure. I thought of different ways to bring in extra income, but most would have limited my freedom and availability to provide hospice and home care services. What I really wanted was a paycheck, not more work. After reading the ads in the Sunday Colorado Springs newspaper for two months and not finding anything flexible enough, I gave up the search.

One day, home alone, I prayed out loud in a rather demanding tone of voice, "God, if you want me out here doing this work, you have to provide a means for me to survive." In no more than thirty seconds the phone rang. It was a School of Nursing faculty member asking if I would be interested in supervising nursing students doing clinical practice at the health department in Colorado Springs. It would be once a week for the spring semester. Wow! It was a perfect answer. How had she known about me? I have no idea, but that was my message not to fear – that my needs would be met. I was a slow learner.

CHAPTER 16

WINTER WENT ON AND ON

t snowed every day in March and into early April. Even die-hard snow lovers were tiring of this incessant daily occurrence. My car was suffering from excessive use. The odometer read well over 100,000 miles by then. A four-wheel-drive vehicle would have been great (and advisable), but I didn't have one. My little Toyota Corolla wagon performed admirably most of the time. And I did indeed have that trusty angel on my shoulder.

March 5, 1983

I'm putting my car in the garage on Friday. The automatic choke is screwed up – only works when the car is warm. Hope I don't need a new one. I've only added one quart of oil in the past two and a half weeks. Guess that problem isn't too bad yet.

March 15, 1983

It's snowing so hard that you can't begin to see across the road and no one is going anywhere. Just what I needed – a day at home. Leigh Anne is here, too – no school. We had about eight inches this morning and over a foot now at 1:00 p.m. Jim has been plowing the parking lot all day, trying to keep up with it. It's getting windy and snow is blowing all over the place. At least it's not too cold: 30 degrees. We're keeping the fire going.

5:00 p.m. – still snowing. Wind has picked up. More snow tonight – blowing and drifting.

Wednesday morning – still snowing. Hard to tell how deep it is – some places one foot, some, two feet. I've just shoveled a path to the car again. Hope I can get out tomorrow.

March 17, 1983

I finally got out of here and made a couple of visits in Green Mountain Falls. Had to walk part way to one. Also had to see someone in Lake George who is really sick with bronchitis. Don't think it's pneumonia. He's too weak to get to the doctor. Hasn't eaten all week, fever, etc. I called tonight and he says he's a little better. It was snowing this morning and again tonight. It snowed the whole time I was in Green Mountain Falls. Only about another inch accumulation. Everyone is getting tired of it. At least the highway was pretty clear today. Everything else is a big mess, and lots of people are still snowed in. More snow coming this weekend.

You know it's cold when…

…you wash the car and the soap freezes on it

…you rinse off the frozen soap and then have to scrape the ice off the windshield before you can drive out of the car wash

...you go out to get some firewood and your damp hair freezes
...you sit on the car seat and it's frozen solid
...getting ready for bed involves taking off 13 things
...your wet laundry freezes in your laundry room before you can get it into the dryer
...the kittens' food freezes faster than they can eat it
...you take off your coat when it finally gets up to 30 degrees
...you have seven blankets on your bed

* * *

Prospect was fortunate to have a staff committed to providing a home care and hospice program tailored to serve the community. It was an opportunity for me to try ideas that had been incubating for years. My greatest frustration was that a day only consisted of 24 hours and I could only work 16 or 18 of them. With staff and volunteers spread out over a 2,000 square mile area, I had not attempted to have a staff meeting. Eventually I decided that I needed them to join me for a brainstorming session. We needed a coherent plan to corral our imaginations. I wanted some ideas other than my own to move the agency ahead.

On the one light snow day in March between two massive snow storms, we met in my living room. I can still see those eight staff and volunteers, some sitting on the floor, all getting acquainted with each other. The energy level was high and enthusiasm contagious. Each expressed his or her interests and ideas. We talked about the eight months since Prospect's inception and what we wanted the coming months and years to look like. We identified program needs and priorities. Particularly important in a rural area with limited resources is having a community health care system with complementary rather than overlapping parts. At that point Prospect was indeed filling a gap in our area's health services. We had the support of local physicians, and the relationships were mutually beneficial. They gave us referrals, and we were their eyes and ears in their patients' homes.

Our staff meeting moved to the topic of ongoing financial sustenance. Because only about half of our expenses were covered by third party reimbursement, we discussed ideas for generating extra income, including grants from foundations, donations from local businesses, and workshops on subjects of professional and personal interest that would be offered to the public. All of these ideas eventually materialized.

Prospect was well established with a Board of Directors, Medical Director, and a staff of all disciplines needed to provide comprehensive home care and hospice services throughout our area. Eventually, we would need better office space and a secretary, but for a fledgling organization, we were well-equipped. As we cared for more patients and families, word of our services spread. We were part of our community and made ourselves available to help in some unusual situations. One morning at 8:30 my phone rang. A man (not one of our patients) had died at home, and the family had no idea what to do with his body, so I went to help and advise them. We offered our nurses and volunteers to the emergency room to assist a family after a traumatic death or serious accident. Prospect had come to be known as a valuable and respected resource.

* * *

On March 31 we had a storm that was starting to melt at around 11:00 a.m. when I left Woodland Park to visit a Cripple Creek hospice patient. The highway from Divide to Cripple Creek had been clear for miles. Approaching the curve at the old town site of Gillette, known for collecting blowing snow, I slowed, having noticed a covering of snow on the road. As I entered the curve, I sensed sideways motion. A strong gust of wind had hit me broadside and sent the car sailing across the ice that was lurking beneath the snow. Fortunately, as I crossed the oncoming lane, no one was coming toward me. A thick curtain of snow flew in front of the car, and it came to rest twenty feet off the road in three feet of snow. With the car tipped at an awkward angle toward the driver's side and the door buried, I climbed out on the passenger side and plodded through hip-deep snow up the bank and onto the road.

The first two cars I flagged down were loaded with tourists and were no help. The third driver suggested that I try the house about 50 yards down the road. The wind was almost more than I could walk against, but I arrived, breathless, at the front door. Before I could knock, the door was opened by a lady who aimed me to the phone on the wall, beside which was posted the number for the tow truck. I was her second visitor that morning and apparently one of many during the snowy winter, day and night.

While waiting for the tow truck, I asked this elderly couple how long they had lived there, and, as I did with anyone who had been around for a long time, mentioned the names of my relatives. Yes, they had known Laura Witcher and Si Pinion. They were glad to meet me and hear about what I was doing, so once again I was less of a stranger because of the good fortune of having had relatives who preceded me.

While we were talking, we looked out of the window just in time to see another vehicle slide off the curve and land precariously close to my car. The tow truck had two vehicles to extricate. As the driver said, "When the wind hits you on that ice, you can't do a thing." Later that afternoon at my Cripple Creek destination, I heard that several other vehicles had slid into the same ditch. It was a good day for the towing business. I opted for the dirt road to Florissant for my trip home. One slide off the road in a day was one too many, and the unpaved road offered more for tires to grip than did the pavement.

CHAPTER 17

Springtime In The Rockies

April 8, 1983

I'm almost afraid to say it, but this might be the first day in six weeks that it hasn't snowed. We got two or three inches yesterday and last night, but it is gorgeous today with a high around 40. The forecast is for warming over the weekend. The mud will be awful. I've had a couple of "hairy" trips to Cripple Creek in this week's snows but no more slides off the road. This morning the highway was solid ice. For the past two days I've had to whack away at the ice caked under my fenders with a hatchet and a pick. I still can't make a hard right turn and my shocks have been frozen solid for three days now. Makes the trips on the dirt roads a bit rough, as they're all a bunch of potholes now anyway.

9:00 p.m. – Well, I spoke too soon. We had a lulu of a snowstorm in Green Mountain Falls this afternoon – right when I needed to be making visits. I made one and then couldn't get up the road to the next. By next winter, I'm going to have a four-wheel-drive vehicle.

Before the Green Mountain Falls visit, a home health aide and I went together to a new patient in an area about seven miles northwest of Woodland Park. They had at least two feet of snow back in there and we had to walk about a quarter mile down their road. The aide lives back in the same area and hasn't been able to drive into her driveway for over two months.

After the spring snows, daytime temperatures were warm enough to thaw the ground and produce the worst mud I had ever seen, much less attempted to drive in. The unpaved roads were a nightmare. On one particularly memorable occasion, I was on my way to Guffey. For almost a week I had been trying to visit a new cancer patient who reportedly had only a short time to live. His wife had discouraged my visits due to the deep snow in their long driveway. Fortunately, they had a phone, so I was able to make medication adjustments and help her with suggestions to keep her husband comfortable. I wanted to meet the patient and his wife and assess his condition firsthand.

The day I decided to make the visit was beautiful – bright blue sky against the white snow and the splendor of Pikes Peak. Soon, however, I was totally focused on the road in front of me. In the best of weather the dirt road to Guffey was a teeth-jarring experience. On this day, however, I was hubcap deep in a quagmire of thick brown soup. Driving on snow was a joy compared to this. I aimed for the few shady spots where the snow lingered, but they were all too few. Sliding in that mud was like being pitched about in a small boat on rough water. From rut to rut I slid. Why I didn't end up in the ditch, I'll never know.

Must have been my angel. Indeed there were some close calls. I held my breath the few times that another vehicle approached. Fully expecting the mush at the sides of the road to suck me up and swallow me, I dared not try to turn around. Though the windshield was plastered with a brown coating, I had no choice but to keep going. My worst fear was getting stuck and having to get out of the car and step in the muck. I could only imagine cold mud oozing over my boot tops.

On the narrow road where the patient lived, the mud was even worse and the road climbed uphill. At a higher elevation, however, the mud changed to snow (whew), so I parked on the road and walked in to the house through deep snow. The choice was a no-brainer. A hike in the snow was hands down better than getting stuck and waiting hours for a tow truck to come to Guffey. The effort in getting to this patient was more than worthwhile and resulted in a most interesting visit.

Roy casually told his wife and me, "Something very strange happened Saturday night. I think I'm making some kind of a transition. I had a dream that the angels of the Lord were above me, up near the ceiling in the four corners of my room. I woke up Sunday morning and my pain was gone, and I've felt better ever since. And I had the same dream Monday and Tuesday nights." I asked Roy what he thought the dream was telling him. He replied with absolute certainty that "the Lord had taken away his disease." His wife expressed surprise at this comment, as apparently Roy had not been a churchgoer and had never spoken of any religious beliefs.

In the next breath he said that he needed to do some woodworking projects and butcher game for his neighbors. Trying to process what Roy was saying, I wasn't sure how to respond, as I doubted that he would be around much longer, much less in any shape to do the tasks he had mentioned. He had the wizened countenance of one whose body was ravaged by advanced cancer. The secretions in his throat attested to the fact that he was not mistaken about the transition that was underway. I was surprised that this retired meat cutter with no interest in spiritual issues would even speak of "making a transition," but he was definitely aware, on some level, of what was happening to him. To my mind, his spirit had already separated from a diseased body and was moving on. Roy talked in a raspy voice of days past and days to come. I wondered what his next calling would be – butcher, woodworker, or something he had never imagined.

Observers of someone undergoing the transition from this life to the next may be puzzled, mystified, or even fascinated by the process underway. I would be remiss in pretending to understand what is going through a patient's mind or even the context of his or her statements. But I have observed that rather than being upsetting or confusing to the patient, the words seem to make total sense. I have never believed, as some medical professionals have concluded, that these transitional conversations are induced either by drugs or oxygen depletion. In Roy's case, he was out of pain and off of all drugs. He knew exactly what he was talking about.

In the hour that I was in Roy's home, a few sunny spots on the road had begun to dry, but only a few. Seeing the sheriff's deputy approaching on the Guffey Road, I flagged him down and asked if he could suggest a better way out.

He shook his head and looked at me like I was crazy for being on that road, especially without four-wheel drive. I drove on. As luck would have it, the only garbage truck I had seen since moving to the mountains greeted me at the crest of a muddy hill. There wasn't room for both of us. The driver stopped and sat there. Was this a stand-off or what? Reluctantly, I backed down the hill. After the road hog passed, I somehow got moving again. Later I learned that the mailman was unable to make the Guffey circuit that day. He should have gone with me!

Spring Thaw

CHAPTER 18

LIFE IS SHORT

In May I had a sad and unsettling experience caring for two young women, both in their thirties, who died within a week of each other. These untimely deaths were a jolting reminder that life can be short – *really* short. The first, Joyce, and her husband had been at M.D. Anderson Cancer Center in Houston, Texas off and on for three years, during which she had received a bone marrow transplant for leukemia. Having learned that the transplant was unsuccessful and that she had no further treatment options, Joyce and her husband were returning to Lake George. I anticipated having her as a hospice patient. On the initial visit, intending to do paperwork necessary for opening a patient record, I encountered a person who was certain that God was going to heal her. I decided to forego the whole admission process and instead, we just visited. I listened to her account of her illness, the extended treatment in Houston, and her anticipation of a miraculous healing. Later, her husband arrived with a friend and the discussion turned to casual conversation.

Several days later I visited Joyce again. The subject of God and healing resurfaced. Because the oncologists had no other treatment to offer, Joyce saw this as an opportunity for God to perform a miracle, which in her mind meant that she would be cured of leukemia. She was a woman of great faith. Not wanting Joyce to think that God was failing her, I guided our discussion in the direction of various kinds of healing – that her perception of healing and God's might not be the same in this situation.

My personal belief is that there comes a point when shedding a worn out or diseased body is not only timely, but God's gift. Joyce seemed to accept this idea as well as understanding that her healing might come in a form other than what she had in mind. Before I left, she wanted me to walk with her up the hill behind the house into the national forest. I wondered how someone in the late stages of leukemia would have enough stamina to walk up a snowy hill at 9,000 feet, but I agreed to go with her. She did amazingly well while I, in my slick-soled western boots, struggled to keep my footing. That afternoon Joyce, evidently at peace with her waning life on earth, progressed into leukemia's final stages and was taken to the hospital in Colorado Springs where she died two weeks later in the arms of her husband. She was healed.

The previous story attests to the importance of understanding where a patient is spiritually and supporting his or her belief system. If a patient is struggling with spiritual issues, clergy may offer help. Often, however, people derive comfort from simply having an opportunity to have conversations about death, the talks that family often shy away from. When family members have encouraged the patient to "keep fighting," the patient may hesitate to express his or her wish to be freed from a cancer-ridden body, lest that appear to be giving up. Involving family members in these talks can be very relieving and can free a dying person from attempts to hang on for the sake of loved ones. Guilt often rears its ugly head – things done and not done, past foibles and squabbles, worries about those who will be left behind. As each issue is acknowledged and dealt with, healing of old wounds takes place. Then the patient and family can move toward acceptance of impending death in a manner consistent with their spiritual and religious beliefs.

CHAPTER 19:

FAMILY CAREGIVING

The second of these young patients, Karen, had a 15-month-old daughter, a best friend who lived nearby, and a devoted husband who felt displaced by the patient's mother, who had come from elsewhere in the state to care for her dying daughter. The mom's presence was constant, upstaging the husband and greatly altering the usual pattern of family functioning. She frequently criticized care given by Karen's husband and managed to alienate him to the point that he sought solace at work. The distraught mother was desperate for control in a situation where control was about as far from possible as was saving her daughter's life. It was a troubling scenario. While Karen hung onto a thread of life, conflict affected the entire situation. As much as I tried to calm the storm, I could not change its course. Nothing could have allayed the distress of this nearly frantic mother who was agonizing at the thought of losing her daughter. My heart went out to these grieving people who were coping in the only way they knew how.

Togetherness and cooperation, or at least tolerance and patience, among family members are assets in hospice caregiving, but such drama as this was not uncommon. Each family member deals with the stress of impending death in his or her own way. One person's approach may conflict with another's and cause tension and even flaring tempers. Hospice workers are often confronted with such situations. In addition to the dying patient, the family, with varying emotional and sometimes physical needs, is also a focus of care, particularly as caregivers become exhausted from trying to meet the patient's increasing and unrelenting needs.

In frequent visits to this home over a three month period, this mother, trying to care for her daughter and granddaughter and manage the household, was losing steam. Friends' and neighbors' assistance was helpful, especially with food and babysitting, but the mother, who was trying to be all and do all, would not leave her daughter's side. Rather than impose pressure on her to take a break and let others relieve her, I backed off and tried to support Karen's husband, who was at a loss as to how to deal with his mother-in-law. The tension in this situation never abated.

Karen's father took a leave of absence from work and came to be with his daughter in her final weeks. He was especially helpful in lifting Karen in and out of the bed and bathtub. With her body reduced to skin and bone (literally), a soak in the tub relieved pressure on bony prominences, and she was comfortable lying in the warm water. The little house was crowded to the max. People were coming and going. The baby needed attention. The mother was reaching her limits.

During Karen's last two weeks, I visited every day, and as the end drew near I stayed in hour-by-hour telephone contact. Then came the day that telephone service was out. At about 9:00 p.m., with phone service not yet restored, my intuition told me to go. Karen died quietly at 11:30 p.m., surrounded by her parents and husband, who had just come in from his evening shift. The scene was at last calm and peaceful. No more struggling, just quiet resignation to a sad event. I left after the mortuary removed the body several hours later, hoping the family might get a few hours of sleep – at least until the baby woke up.

This situation left me with mixed feelings. I had hoped for some resolution of conflicts, but it didn't happen. I wondered if anything would have helped. On the way home at 4:00 a.m., bleary-eyed and fighting to stay awake, I detected a large mass in the inky darkness of the road to Florissant. My tired eyes made out a huge herd of elk that owned the road. In a fifteen-minute wait for them to move on, I rehashed the evening's events and unwound from a drama that ended as well as probably possible in spite of tense weeks leading up to Karen's death.

Family functioning intrigued me. At times, I felt as if I were directing a reality play with each actor playing a part that evolved as the story unfolded. With no lines to memorize, it was an impromptu performance. The actors would at times be angry or sad, sometimes beg for the end to come, and oftentimes, be overcome with fatigue and frustration. Each moved offstage at one time or another as personal needs dictated, but all came together for the final curtain call. Relatives from "back east" (or anywhere else) were often an added challenge. They would appear on the scene near the end with all manner of advice for family caregivers who had been performing admirably for some time. Resolving some of the resulting bones of contention usually involved defusing tensions and was an expected part of the process. The family (whoever that happened to be, related or not) was key to the success of home care. Because nursing, personal care, and therapy services were intermittent, having one or more caregivers in the home was an essential piece of a care plan. In the case of hospice, an inpatient alternative was a certification requirement and was to be used in case of family burnout, a patient without a caregiver, or a pain management problem. Prospect had an agreement with a nursing facility in Colorado Springs for such a need, but it was never used. Our patients wanted to be at home, and we did our best to keep them there.

I have utmost respect for families that are willing to care for a chronically ill or dying person at home. It is a huge job. There are understandable frustrations such as trying to prepare food to appeal to a waning appetite and trying to keep a thin, frail body comfortable in a bed or recliner. Patience is indeed a virtue when nothing seems to satisfy. A patient's days and nights may be reversed, and caregivers long for a night of sleep. Home care requires a willingness to learn and carry out nursing procedures and provide personal care to a bedbound patient. It is physically taxing. And to be sure, bathing and diapering an incontinent adult is a far cry from caring for a cute little baby.

Having more than one caregiver was always a plus. Even though friends, neighbors and hospice volunteers were available to give a caregiver a break or a much needed nap, by the time a patient died, a family was usu-ally exhausted. It often seemed that as caregivers were reaching their limit, the patient died – almost as if accom-modating their need. After a death, I did my best to help the family understand that their relief was totally appro-priate and that they should feel proud of their accom-plishment and their gift to a loved one.

I remember one situation that took a toll on the primary caregiver, who happened to be a near-elderly daughter-in-law. Julia was a prim and proper lady in her upper eighties who had pneumonia in addition to being generally weak from other medical problems. She did not want to be hospitalized for her pneumonia. Being a former hat-and-glove southern lady who was used to having "help," she found great pleasure in residing with her son and his wife and receiving all the attention she desired. I worked on resolving the pneumonia, and the daughter-in-law provided personal care and meals to Julia, who divided her time between bed and wheel-chair. The exhausted caregiver ended up in bed with a back strain, attesting to the physical stress of lengthy caregiving. This turn of events brought Julia's son out of the woodwork. Finding that the caregiver role was no walk in the park, he decided to place his mother, kick-ing and screaming, in the Cripple Creek nursing home. Indeed, home care has its limits and is not always a feasi-ble choice. I visited this lady (and she *was* a lady) when I happened to be in Cripple Creek. She was not at all happy in her new environment, but she was in the right place. She needed a staff of workers.

CHAPTER 20

HOME DEATH

As difficult as it is to be a caregiver, being the dying person is no easy assignment either. Except in the case of sudden death, dying may be a protracted process wrought with pain and struggles of an emotional and physical nature. Hospices today offer sedation, oxygen, and medications (in addition to narcotics for pain management) to control symptoms common to dying patients – agitation, secretions in the throat, and sonorous respirations – all of which may be unsettling to surrounding family. The approach in the early years was to let the dying process play out naturally and to prepare the family for the symptoms and behaviors that usually occur as life is ebbing. Whenever possible, a nurse would be present during the final hours to reassure the family that the different phases they were observing were normal. As prepared as a family may be, actually witnessing the dying process, especially in someone they love, is a time of needed support. Watchful waiting, sometimes seemingly endless, through long nights, is common.

At the near-end stage, and sometimes for several days prior, the patient is detaching from this world. It is important for family caregivers to understand this part of the process, which sometimes seems hallucinatory. A faraway look is a clue, as are conversations with those who have gone before. This vacillation between planes is fascinating to those of us who have spent time with dying people. When a person near death seems to be hanging onto life, he or she may be waiting for an event, a certain person to arrive, or something unidentifiable. In that case, I would ask the family if they had any idea what the patient was waiting for and if they had given him or her permission to go. Sometimes a near-death patient is reluctant to leave a spouse or other dependent person and needs to hear reassurance that the one(s) left behind will be cared for. Encouragement to "go to the light" or to "go to _____" (a relative or spouse already deceased) is sometimes meaningful to a patient, especially one who musters strength to repeatedly reach upward. Reports from people who have had near-death experiences often include going toward a bright light and seeing deceased friends or relatives.

Even though the patient may seem to be disconnected from reality, those around him or her can be assured that hearing usually remains intact and the presence of loved ones continues to be important. Sitting at the bedside, talking in normal tones, singing favorite songs or hymns, and holding a hand or gently touching a shoulder are all appropriate and serve to ease the process of passing. Some families dim the lights, light candles, and play soft music. Usually, by that time, pain is no longer an issue, and there is no need to offer food or water. A dry mouth and lips can be swabbed with a soft, dampened cloth. The final moments, when respirations are purely mechanical (no active patient control) and are becoming irregular and widely spaced, are, in my opinion, the family's time. I usually stepped into the background for the moment when life ended.

Death with dignity is an often-used phrase. I'm not sure that I would classify the dying process as being especially dignified, regardless of intentions. Rather it seems more important to aspire to a goal of ensuring a setting in which a person is honored and respected to the end, when bodies are reduced to basic functions. No matter what physical attributes are compromised in final days, the patient remains the person he or she was throughout life. In situations where the dying person was the "black sheep of the family," or perhaps had less than ideal relationships with other members, he or she is nevertheless entitled to kindness and compassionate care from those who have the ability to forego judgment and overlook past mistakes.

Pet behavior around a sick or dying person is fascinating. Dogs, especially, sense that something unusual is going on. They know that things aren't as they should be. People are coming and going. Nights are interrupted with activity surrounding a sick person, who may not be sleeping in his or her own bed.

Bill was a hospice patient whose large, extended family lived nearby, so extra people were almost always at the house, sharing caregiving with the patient's wife. He was in a hospital bed in the middle of the living room.

Bill's little dog, his constant companion, took up residence under the bed. Substantial cajoling was required to get the dog to go outside or to go to the kitchen to eat. They resorted to placing the dog's food and water under the bed. When Bill died we all noticed that at the precise moment of his last breath, the dog, sensing that, ran to the back bedroom and hid under the bed. Pets want to be with their person as much as the owner wants to be with the pet. The love goes both ways. And pets do grieve their losses.

When death occurred, the family needed time to see and accept the finality of the event – that this thing that had totally consumed them and all of their energies was really over. It was a powerful moment. If a family member wished to assist me in bathing and dressing the body and possibly changing the sheets, I was thankful for the help. Dead weight is just that. Even an emaciated body is heavy. Timing of the call to the mortuary was up to the family. Some wanted the body removed as soon as possible. Others preferred to wait for other family to arrive or were in no hurry for reasons of their own.

The wonderful men at Blount Mortuary on the west side of Colorado Springs, our usual resource, were always on call and came out on many a frigid night, dressed impeccably in suits and ties. Because of our location, we usually had a couple of hours to wait, time for the family to say their final goodbyes. Sitting with the family while waiting for the mortuary, we talked about their caregiving experience and the patient's life. It was a quiet, peaceful end to a great effort. I tried to assist the morticians whenever and however I could. Often a little cabin or a 100-year-old dwelling was inhospitable to a gurney, so we had to carry the body to it from a bedroom, through a narrow hall, and sometimes outside. Occasionally family members helped, but for some, the removal of their loved one from the home was a tough moment, and they preferred to be in another room. Afterwards I tried to straighten the area where the patient had been, strip the bed, and dispose of caregiving supplies and medications, especially narcotics, which were not left in a home for safety reasons. When that was done and the family seemed to be settled, I left, usually with a sigh of relief. Mission accomplished.

Normally an unattended death required a coroner call, but in the case of an expected home death when the physician had agreed to sign the death certificate, the coroner did not need to come and the mortuary could remove the body. When a home death was anticipated, all of these contacts and arrangements were made ahead of time. In a situation where the nurse was not present when death occurred, the family was instructed *not* to call 911, as the first responders would be obligated to attempt resuscitation. Instead, they were to call their nurse. With everyone apprised of the situation, there were no surprises and no legal problems. The physician was notified as soon as reasonable after the death, on the same day or the following morning if the death occurred during the night.

I recall only one home death that was not ideal. I had suspected that this patient's death might be different from most. She had a neurological condition that was paralyzing her body and would eventually affect her diaphragm and swallowing ability. During the course of her care, there were several times when her anxious husband needed assistance or reassurance. One Sunday afternoon the patient was having breathing problems and I went to the home. I called her physician for advice, and a little while later, he appeared at the door to help resolve the problem. I appreciated his support. Her disease course had been a roller-coaster ride, and we (husband included) knew it was nearing the end. In spite of the patient's breathing and swallowing problems, her husband wanted to keep her at home.

In a middle-of-the-night phone call the distraught, barely understandable husband said that his wife had died and that he was sure he had killed her, because she had choked on a pill he had given her. I jumped out of bed, heart pounding, threw on some clothes, and took off for the home, which was about thirty miles away. Driving as fast as I dared around the curves of Florissant Canyon, I prayed that I could come up with some way to comfort this man. Though this was the anticipated outcome, I was sorry for him that his wife's death occurred as it did. It took this man several weeks and a few reassuring conversations with the physician to believe that it was the progression of the disease that ended his wife's life. If it hadn't been the pill, it would have been the next spoonful of food he had offered her.

In time, he started attending the senior center for a midday meal. There he met a lovely widow whom he married within the year. I had never seen him so happy. It was always encouraging to see someone emerge from grief and move on to a new chapter as a survivor.

CHAPTER 21

FUNERALS AND MEMORIAL SERVICES

Many families opted for the traditional choice of embalming, open casket and viewing, and then a funeral and burial. However, just as many were choosing cremation, with or without embalming and viewing, followed by a memorial service. Some chose to bury the remains, and others preferred to scatter them in a meaningful place. Often, after a protracted illness such as cancer, when a person was emaciated prior to death, a family chose to have a closed casket or direct cremation. Family members didn't always agree on these choices, so making decisions before death, with the patient included in the conversation, was a wise course of action. Family may shy away from having such a discussion, but most people who are dying are very aware that their days are nearing an end, even if family encouraged "hanging on" or "fighting to the end." They welcome an opportunity to make their wishes known. They do want someone to listen to them and if family can't or won't do it, a hospice worker may serve as the listener and then communicate the patient's wishes or better yet, bring family into the conversation. When final wishes are known, arrangements can be made with the funeral home or mortuary before the death occurs. In the case of a direct cremation, signature of more than one family member may be necessary. Once the business of dying has been taken care of, the process of dying can be the total focus.

I attended the funerals and memorial services of all of my patients, unless they occurred out of state, as a gesture of support for the family. At some the family asked me to sit with them or to say a few words. Most families found the day of the service to be very stressful and felt that it was a major hurdle to conquer, after which they could begin putting their lives back together. They were exhausted after being caregivers, and the added impact of dealing with relatives from out of town, food from friends and neighbors (and nowhere to put all of it), telephone calls and visits, and sleep deprivation only added another level of fatigue and often, stress. Some people needed a formal service to signify completion or finality of life. Others, often granting the wishes of the dying person, chose to have no service. For the families involved, that decision seemed to be a relief. They could avoid an event that would add to their exhaustion. Having a memorial service at some later date was a common compromise that gave caregivers time to heal but also provided distant family and acquaintances an opportunity to gather and pay tribute to the person who had gone on.

Caregivers needed care and support through the initial after-death period, so I continued to view the family as a patient for at least several weeks, even if a bereavement volunteer had begun visiting. Having survived the immediate aftermath, the family faced a period of busyness with financial and legal affairs needing to be handled – death certificates, insurance policies, pensions, social security, bank accounts, bills, and so on – always encountering a few frustrating snags. At the one-month point, caregivers were still exhausted, and it was an important time for a visit. It was the beginning of a readily apparent letdown. Much of the business had been taken care of by then, contacts from friends and relatives were less frequent, and the time had come to deal with the grieving process.

CHAPTER 22

EXPERIENCING GRIEF

When someone dies, others are left behind to carve out life in a new form. The loss deprives survivors of someone they depended on, cared deeply for, and maybe partnered with. It may have been a child, sibling, parent, spouse or other closely connected person. The death may reconfigure a family and cause roles to change. Death of parents moves each generation up a level. Death of a child denies parenthood. A spouse's death means one will no longer be a husband or wife but instead, a widow or widower, designations that are unwelcome and hard to get used to. Suddenly finding oneself living alone requires major adjustments. Any one of these identity alterations causes a significant life change not of one's choosing and gives reason to grieve. Denying grief or trying to force it into hiding serves only to prolong it.

Grief done right takes time and patience. The first year following a death is a survival experience, living through holidays, birthdays, anniversaries, and even the four seasons for the first time without this person who is no longer physically present. Beyond that year, for whatever time is needed to resolve lingering issues, grief continues in a variety of forms. The function of grief – and yes, it does have purpose – is to give a survivor time to sort through memories and select those to hold onto. Not-so-good memories such as relationship difficulties, detrimental behavior choices, and even the image of a loved one in a state of physical decline eventually take a back seat to more positive memories. Grief is a period of release and restoration. Conversations with the deceased – not all pleasant – help the process move forward. These monologues serve to dispel lingering anger and to express sadness and frustration at being left behind. There are ups and downs – two steps forward, one step back. There is no time limit for grief.

I made a bereavement visit to a lady whose husband had died several months previously. She had resumed her usual activities and was adjusting admirably to a single life. The day of my visit she was in tears and said that it was "just a bad day." Further elaboration revealed that she had been cleaning house and had found a few strands of her husband's hair. She melted. Grief is anything but a steady climb. As a poignant reminder of its presence and power, it gives an occasional tap on a survivor's shoulder, dredging up yet another memory to find its place in the storehouse of a past life.

Love does not die. Even when a widow or widower remarries, the new relationship necessarily shares space with a past life and a previous love. Healthy grieving does not mean forgetting. The concept of closure following a death baffles me. It doesn't happen. And why should it? Even many years after a loved one's death, there is a lingering void. A new relationship does not replace a lost one. Choosing to love again following the death of a spouse is a bold step and is evidence of both healthy grieving and the desire for another close relationship. Since grief may continue to rear its head at unexpected times, the new partner can play an important supporting role in helping the survivor to move ahead in a life yet to be lived.

Counseling is appropriate in the case of prolonged despondency or unresolved and unrelenting grief that seems to have taken over a survivor's life. A bereavement volunteer or a grief group often helps people move through the grieving process, realizing they are not alone on their journey and finding that the "down" days will become fewer and farther between.

CHAPTER 23

FUNDING

Obtaining funding for not-for-profit hospice and home care programs was (and still is) a challenge requiring ongoing effort. Third party reimbursement – Medicare, Medicaid, private insurance – pays only part of the cost of a home care visit and a federally-determined per diem cost of hospice care. The problem with the hospice stipend is that care is more expensive during a patient's final days, when visits are frequent, but often a hospice referral doesn't materialize until the end of life is near. Admitting a hospice patient soon after a prognosis of six months to live or less (which is always a guess) is a boon to the hospice as well as the patient and family, both financially and emotionally. Having time to establish a relationship benefits the family and hospice workers. Dying is often a lengthy process, not simply an event. Once that process has begun and the end is anticipated, understood, and planned for, the patient and family can go on living the remainder of their lives together with as much quality as is possible. The family and patient benefit from services, equipment, and medication provided by hospice, and the hospice benefits from days of receiving the per diem payment for a time before the patient needs intense care and daily visits.

Nevertheless, reimbursement in the case of both home care and hospice services does not cover an agency's administrative costs – staffing, management, compliance with regulations, travel, office, and so on. While financial solvency was a never-ending struggle, patient care reigned as Prospect's number one focus and priority. Paperwork, the nemesis of every business, was a nagging distraction. Patient records – documentation to satisfy requirements of third party payors, especially Medicare, were a necessary component of care. Under the home care program regulations, a visit was incomplete without documentation that reflected a skilled level of nursing care or therapy, homebound status of the patient, and instability of his or her condition.

Picky Medicare home care reviewers made unannounced visits to the agency to devour patient charts searching for the least reason to deny services already provided and paid for, if records lacked appropriate verbage. Denials meant having to refund to the government money previously reimbursed to the agency and long since disbursed to cover wages and other expenses. It was an ongoing threat. A Medicare-funded home care patient needed to evidence improvement or decline – never maintaining status quo. If a recovering stroke patient walked twenty feet today, he or she had to walk farther the next visit, or the subsequent visit would not be covered (paid for). If a congestive heart failure patient's symptoms subsided for two visits in a row, he or she had to be discharged, as Medicare would no longer pay. Indeed, this little agency was saving the government thousands of dollars by keeping patients at home rather than in expensive inpatient facilities such as hospitals and nursing homes, but maintaining a patient at an optimal level was out of the question. If a home care patient stabilized, the case had to be closed and reopened at a later date, when a downturn occurred.

Home care has been documented repeatedly as a cost-saving measure, with prevention of crises and subsequent hospitalizations as a major goal. Unfortunately, Medicare was not designed to address prevention. Not only was that approach inefficient, it went against the core of my public health background, where prevention is the primary goal. Another problematic issue with Medicare home care reimbursement was the method of determining the cost of home visits, the basis for an agency's payments. For some ridiculous reason, rural costs were deemed to be less than the expense of providing care in a metropolitan area. Did the policymakers have any idea of rural travel expenses? Apparently not.

In addition to reimbursement for services, funding for not-for-profit agencies comes from grants, fundraising events, and contributions. Fundraising in rural areas often does not produce significant amounts of money, but exposure and publicity, rather than cash, were the payoffs for Prospect. Securing grants required hours of compiling data and supporting documents plus narrative about the program as requested by the grantor. Nevertheless, it proved to be a worthwhile undertaking for Prospect in the first and subsequent years.

I applied for a U.S. Public Health Service grant for agency start-up funding. My father had learned about the grant through an announcement in the *Congressional Record*, and he encouraged me to apply. The required documentation to support the request (statistics and narrative) had been written and photocopied piecemeal over a period of weeks prior to the midnight postmark deadline on June 30, 1983. I needed to provide three sets of the documents. By the afternoon of the due date, I had photocopied all of it and purchased three large envelopes, but the submissions had not been collated. Late that evening, I raced down to the one post office in Colorado Springs that was open at night. Feeling as if I were running a marathon and with about that much adrenaline pumping, I stood at a table in the post office, separated my huge pile of papers into three sets, and stuffed them into envelopes as the deadline approached. As luck would have it, the postmarking and stamping machine was out of order. The slow-moving attendant on duty casually went to the back room, located a hand stamp, and set it to the time and date. Then the envelopes had to be weighed and stamps purchased. I was really squirming as I watched the minutes tick by. At 11:45 p.m. my envelopes were finally postmarked, stamped and in the mail. I defended the grant request before a board of government officials in Denver, and secured $33,700 from which I wrote my first salary check.

With more hospice patients being cared for, memorial contributions following patient deaths became a substantial part of Prospect's income. As word spread about this unique agency providing care in the mountains, it was publicized not only in local newspapers but also in the Colorado Springs *Gazette Telegraph*. A reporter rode with me to visit several patients (with prior approval) and produced a two-page article with photographs that put Prospect on the map. Contributions arrived from donors outside the area with no connection other than a desire for the agency's success.

CHAPTER 24

NEW BEGINNINGS

My first year in the mountains was drawing to a close. Prospect was launched, and Leigh Anne and I survived. When the spring thaw finally arrived and the snow melted, an amazing amount of firewood appeared, as if the wood pile in front of the house had regenerated. I had no idea that so much firewood had been buried beneath the snow.

June 16, 1983
Our weather is finally beginning to warm up – only in the daytime though. We've had freezes three nights this week. I typed until 1:00 this morning, and by the time I got to bed I was so cold that my quilt and seven blankets didn't do a thing – even after a cup of hot tea – so I got up and put on wool sox and my bedroom slippers. Already had on my long, hooded sweatshirt-nightgown and a T-shirt. Hard to believe for June 15th. At least the days are warm and the aspens are finally getting green leaves.

As the year ended, my life was about to undergo another major change. A romantic relationship was brewing. Given that I had no interest in dating or any time for a social life other than the local dances, this turn of events was quite unexpected. To say that our meeting was unconventional is an understatement. Budd Rice was the husband of Joyce, the first of the two young women to die in the same week – the one who expected the miraculous healing of her leukemia. Since the family lived near me, south of Lake George, I served as the bereavement volunteer following Joyce's death. Even though Joyce had never received actual hospice care, it was common for Prospect to offer support to bereaved families. I was especially concerned about this situation, as Joyce had a twelve-year-old daughter whose life had been turned upside down by lengthy trips to Texas for the three years of her mother's treatment and then finally, by her mother's death. Budd's son had been shuffled from one neighbor to the next in order to remain in his school in Fairplay during that time.

As the weeks went on, bereavement contacts turned into lengthy phone calls. A mutual attraction was apparent, but I was horrified that I might let a personal relationship with someone in a hospice family confound my professional endeavors. Budd took me on an outing that we now call our one and only date. It was a group event – a picnic in Cripple Creek. The chaplain from M. D. Anderson Hospital in Houston had come to Colorado with his wife and daughter to see how Budd was doing. Budd had lived with the chaplain's family during times when Joyce was in the hospital there, and they had formed a close relationship. Budd wanted me to meet them and to take a day off, my first since Christmas.

June 23, 1983

Will be going to Donkey Derby Day in Cripple Creek on Saturday, then to a play in Fairplay that evening. One of my friends wrote it, and I know it will be funny. I have no business taking a day and night off this weekend, but those are both things I don't want to miss. I'm going to Cripple Creek with the guy who fixed my speedometer cable, his wife's daughter, and the hospital chaplain from Houston and his wife and daughter. We are taking a picnic and going up around some old mines to cook our food and hike around a little. Depends on how the Texans do at 10,000 feet. Anyway, it will be a fun day.

The wildflowers have started to bloom this week. We've had some warm weather, also some thunderstorms last night. The electricity went off at 9:00 p.m. and didn't come back on till 12:30 a.m. I typed by my oil lamps. I don't see how Lincoln read by candle light all the time.

July 1, 1983

I probably shouldn't have taken last Saturday off to go to Cripple Creek with Budd Rice and the chaplain and his family, but it was a great day. They were super people. We really had fun poking around Cripple Creek and Victor, visiting an old mine, cooking hamburgers off in a deserted place, etc. Then we went out to eat in Fairplay and went to that good play. It was really one of the most relaxing days I've had all year (Yes, it's been one year today), so I can't really say I regret taking the time.

I really liked Budd and respected the way he had handled his wife's illness and death, plus the issues surrounding the children's wellbeing, but he wasn't exactly someone I envisioned myself with. I had frequent heart-to-heart conversations with God, like, "What is going on here? How could this be happening?" I tried to talk myself out of the whole idea of getting involved in a relationship. The response was unmistakable. A distinct voice from somewhere replied, "You are going to be married to this man." I just about choked. Where did *that* voice come from? Was there someone else in the room? I looked around, but I was alone.

I replied to the voice, as if to set things straight, "This man is not my type."

And again some days later, the same voice said, "He is going to be your husband."

I found this possibility rather hard to believe, but the voice and the words were undeniable. Budd was pretty rough around the edges, always in western boots and a cowboy hat that didn't quite cover his mop of red hair. A bushy red beard and mustache hid all but a freckled nose and two piercing eyes. He drove an old rough-riding Ford Bronco that I learned on our drive to Fairplay required manual operation of the windshield wipers by the person in the passenger seat.

Budd was raised on a farm in the San Luis Valley in southern Colorado. A farm boy. His family's place sounded to me like Old MacDonald's farm: sheep, pigs, horses, cows, goats, cats, dogs, ducks, chickens, geese, a pet magpie, and an injured golden eagle in rehabilitation. Between a large garden and their livestock, there was no shortage of food. They ate what they produced. In Budd's family, schoolwork took a backseat to farm chores, which for him included milking 20 cows every morning and evening, plowing and planting in springtime, and cutting and stacking hay in the fall. Summers found him on his horse, either herding 50 head of cattle, his summer job, or riding and camping with his best friend Stan Stahl in what is now Great Sand Dunes National Park. At one point the Rice's small house was popping at the seams with two parents, three children, two grandchildren, and three orphaned cousins. With nothing more than building instructions provided by his dad before leaving for work in the mornings, Budd and his mother constructed an addition to the house.

Our upbringings could not have been any less similar. In my home, schoolwork took priority over everything else. The milkman delivered milk. Food came from the Safeway. We paid to take rides on horses – first on tethered ponies that walked around in a circle at a pony ring that came to town on Sundays and later at nearby riding stables. I grew up watching cowboys on television and imagining life in the West. Budd grew up with the real thing. Spin and Marty, the lead teenage characters on a dude ranch segment of the Mickey Mouse Club television show were the heart throbs of my junior high school girlfriends and me. Cowboys were fantasized by girls in the east, and here I was – about to lay claim to one of my own.

As our relationship developed, we realized that though our backgrounds were very different, our values were on the same page. His devotion to Joyce and unrelenting care during her illness were impressive. Later on Budd told me that sometime during the last week of her life Joyce had suggested that he marry me. Budd was taken aback at such an idea, especially because at that point he barely knew me, and then only as "the hospice nurse." We both were flabbergasted at this unfolding situation. And I was afraid. Afraid of what people would think. Afraid of the effect on my daughter and Budd's stepdaughter. Afraid of trying to combine my all-consuming work with a new marriage. Even afraid of trying another marriage. In time, fear gave way to comfort as I began to accept that I was taking the right step on a very interesting journey – a journey that really wasn't of my own making. It just happened. My doubts vanished.

Mom and Dad had planned to visit Leigh Anne and me in July. Other than telling them about the Cripple Creek picnic, I had made no mention of Budd. They were still trying to get used to my wild adventure, and I didn't want to drop another bomb – at least not yet. But I had to. Budd and I knew where we were headed. He would be a frequent presence during their visit, and of course I wanted them to meet him. I wrote a long letter to my parents before they came. Aside from extolling Budd's virtues, I tried to convince them that neither Budd nor I was jumping into this relationship without many hours of discussion and contemplation. That letter prompted an immediate telephone call that must have been loaded with cautionary comments. My letter that followed, the last one before their visit, was a plea for their support.

July 16, 1983

I could tell by the sound of your voices this morning that your anxiety level is pretty high regarding the direction my life seems to be headed. Please do not worry about me. If I've learned one thing over the years it is how to survive when things don't go the way I'd planned and how to live when they do. I am willing to take risks because I know that's a requirement of living life to the fullest. I do not want to miss anything life has to offer, and I would rather take a chance and go for it than to be sitting in a wheelchair at age 85 wishing I had. I have learned so much from very ill and dying people. I don't want to be one who regrets not having done this or that. To me that means taking calculated risks, knowing that whatever the outcome, I will survive and grow from it.

After the initial shock, they were prepared for the surprising turn of events. The visit went well. This time Dad had a chance to visit the old ranch and surrounding area, and Budd took all of us to the Sand Dunes, his childhood playground. My mother was particularly relieved that I would no longer be floundering around by myself in the mountains, that I would have someone looking out for me. Apparently I had occupied a substantial amount of her prayer time.

When I finally got up my nerve to tell anyone about this unlikely happening, the first person I confided in was Prospect's volunteer coordinator. It was a test to see what kind of response it evoked. I was relieved that she was not horrified. After ascertaining that the feelings were mutual, her reaction was a total thumbs up. "Go for it," she said, and I took her advice.

As word of our pending marriage slipped out and made its way around the area, the reaction was totally heartwarming. Budd's and Joyce's friends were thrilled, as were my co-workers and patients. Even though our plans were known, we thought that we should wait at least six months after Joyce's death to have a wedding. That would have been after November 18. It seemed like the right thing to do.

August 30, 1983

We thought we were keeping such a good secret, but typical of small-town living, the secret isn't one anymore and hasn't been for a few weeks. It's really a relief to have it all out, especially knowing what the reaction has been. Everyone thinks it's wonderful and can't understand why we would want to wait till the end of November. So since we really didn't want to anyway, we changed the date. I think the end of October is long enough to wait. They announced it at Christ Haven, where Budd works, and Budd feels really good because everyone is so happy for him.

Budd and I were married on October 23, 1983, in western clothes and boots in front of the huge stone fireplace at Christ Haven Lodge in Florissant. Reverend Bob Kamrath, the hospital chaplain from Houston, performed our ceremony with about 100 friends and both families in attendance. We learned that after our picnic in Cripple Creek, Bob and his wife and daughter had prayed that Budd and I would get together. They were elated to see Budd moving on to the next chapter of his life after three years of struggling with Joyce's cancer. We honeymooned in a tent, traveling around parts of the southwest that were new to me. I finally had a chance to see the Grand Canyon.

Bride and Groom, Western Style

So Leigh Anne and I moved "even farther into the boonies," as she christened our new home nine miles south of Lake George. I hated to leave the Spigners and the convenience of the little red house and the Ponderosa Store, but the time had come for me to move on to the next chapter of my own unfolding journey. Budd's place on the west side of Pikes Peak abutted the Pike National Forest, beyond which was a former section of Witcher's 76 Ranch. We had the only phone in the area, so our door was always unlocked for the occasional stranded motorist. An unending wood supply was available in the forest, and before winter set in Budd bought a snow plow. There's nothing like a few cords of firewood, split and stacked in the shed, to make winter less intimidating. As a "jack of all trades," Budd was skilled at maintaining and repairing our vehicles and also at building an addition to the house to accommodate our blended family.

Deer and elk hunting, part of Budd's life for many years, became part of mine as well. His wedding gift to me was a rifle. I'm not sure that I ever said, "Thank you." I had never owned a weapon. Saturday, a week before our wedding and the opening day of elk season, was to be my first hunting trip. Not that I planned to shoot at anything. I was only going along for the ride. I left my warm bed at 3:30 a.m., put on plenty of clothes, and drove with the picnic lunch I'd packed out to Budd's place, ready to go hunting at daybreak. Barely awake, I doubted that this was going to be my idea of a good time, but off we went. About a mile from Budd's house there they were – the herd of elk that Budd had spotted several times. I stayed in the Bronco while Budd tromped out into the field and shot a huge bull elk. By 7:30 a.m. he had hauled out the elk and we were back at his house. And that was my big day of hunting. He gutted the elk and let it hang for a week in the freezing temperatures. Then he took it to the Colorado Springs meat processor to be cut up and frozen until we retrieved it after our honeymoon. That one elk provided us with 300 pounds of delicious (better-than-beef) meat that fed our family for two years.

Antelope sausage and venison added to our food supply. I never pulled a trigger on a hunting trip, but on several occasions was called upon to help drag a dead deer out of the woods or up a hill. They always seemed to die in a ravine or on the other side of a fence. As much as I hated the idea of killing those beautiful creatures, I appreciated the huge dent they made in our grocery bill. Neither Budd nor I made much of a salary. He worked part time as the maintenance man at Christ Haven Lodge. He also plowed snow for area residents and did odd jobs like carpentry and plumbing repairs. We had enough money to support our no-frills lifestyle plus an occasional ski trip with the girls. Eating game and heating with wood helped to keep our expenses down.

On snowy winter nights when the moon was full, Budd and I donned our cross-country skis and visited our nearest neighbors who lived a mile and a half away. We had wonderful friends whose lifestyles were similar to our own. Around Christmas time, in a hay wagon hitched to a tractor, a group of us – adults and kids - chugged around the Lake George area Christmas caroling, and then roasted hot dogs over a welcome fire in zero degree weather.

Budd Plowing Our Snow

Cold, snowy winters continued to challenge our existence. The county road at the end of our lane was plowed soon after a storm and Budd kept our driveway open. By the end of winter the snow was piled high, and we had a narrow path with six-foot-high walls of snow on both sides going from our vehicles to the woodshed and on to the back door. Besides cutting wood in the short summer, we went camping when I could get away. Our lives were simple, and life was good. Living in the middle of nowhere was no problem for me, especially with a wonderful husband.

CHAPTER 25

THE SECOND YEAR

Budd became a "Hospice Husband," understanding that there would be times when patients came first, when hospice fund raising activities needed a hand, when the monthly billing was a priority, or when I would be preoccupied with an impending death, sleeping in my clothes with the telephone on the bed. He knew the drill. He was also on hand to transport me to patients' homes in snowstorms in his Bronco with snowplow attached. I bought a much-needed four-wheel-drive vehicle, and Budd installed a block heater that ensured warm start-ups during cold winter months. I was well cared for.

Prospect got a bona fide office – one room and a closet in the Loyd Harmon Construction Company building in Florissant. The $100 per month rent was affordable and included utilities and use of the photocopier. Loyd's secretary had an extension to Prospect's phone and took calls when no one was in the office. The closet stored blank forms, patient and administrative records, and the growing stash of donated home care equipment and supplies. We were caring for more patients, and the staff was expanding to meet the need. Staff meetings were a comical sight, with our group crowded around the only table (a communal desk) and sitting on anything available – wheelchair, bedside commode, shower bench, odd chairs.

As the patient census increased, the need for additional workers was apparent. More nurses, therapists, and aides were hired in both ends of the service area. By the end of the second year, Prospect had approximately twenty staff and volunteers. The addition of staff to meet growing needs created more administrative and supervisory duties, all of which decreased my time available for patients. Knowing that patient care was the source of my own job satisfaction, I was not about to relinquish all involvement with patients and families and succumb to a full time administrative job again. For me, involvement with each patient and family was not only an opportunity to provide a service but also to give something of myself and to know some wonderful, inspiring people.

The business side of providing hospice and home care services, though time consuming, was a necessary evil. In addition to patient records, administrative records of all sorts were necessary: personnel records, payroll, tax withholding and quarterly payments, insurance, quarterly grant reports, documentation of staff meetings and patient reviews to comply with hospice and home care regulations, and monthly billing for services. I was becoming overwhelmed. Hiring help was the obvious solution, but I had not met anyone who seemed like a possible candidate for the office job, and anyway, there wasn't enough cash coming in at that point to pay anyone.

I resorted to doing paperwork most evenings and spending some Saturday and Sunday afternoons in the office to do the billing and other administrative tasks that required peace and quiet. I was busier than ever as the summer of 1984 came to an end, as nurse, administrator, human resources director, accountant, and billing clerk all rolled into one. Was I there for the patients, or was the effort all for Medicare? Sometimes, late at night and bleary-eyed, I wondered. More than once I wished to have done the nursing work as a volunteer and avoided the red tape and voluminous paperwork. Unfortunately, if you didn't play by government rules, you didn't play at all.

CHAPTER 26

MEMORABLE PATIENTS

Determined not to give up patient care entirely, I resorted to carrying a caseload of two or three patients at a time. Dear old Milly was one of these. I didn't dare assign her to anyone else. At almost 90, Milly was the personification of the adage that "the feisty ones live the longest." Her doctor chuckled when he referred her as one of Prospect's first home care patients. She had advanced congestive heart failure and required monitoring to adjust her medications to her frequently changing symptoms. She was clinically unstable, and my stethoscope often magnified the sounds of fluid stalled in her lungs as her heart failure worsened. The goal was to keep her out of the hospital and to control her symptoms.

Milly lived on the side of a steep hill in Green Mountain Falls in a little house she had occupied for many years, formerly with her husband but alone for several years since his death. Set in her ways, cantankerous, and demanding, she embodied many negative characteristics applied to the elderly. But she was a survivor. No longer able to climb the stairs to her bedroom, she slept on her couch. No longer able to get in and out of a bathtub but insisting on doing her own bath, she informed me in her most authoritarian voice that "anything that needs to be washed can be washed at a bathroom sink."

One day as I drew a blood sample for her monthly digitalis level she, in her animated way of talking, raised her hands, dislodging the needle from her vein and relocating it in my thigh. She just kept right on talking. Milly had a way of getting what she wanted. Granting her wishes was far easier than arguing with her – and losing. Her housekeeper often shook her head at each new and unusual request, such as retrieving all of the stale donuts from the grocery store in large garbage bags and tearing them, gooey and sometimes jelly-filled, into bite-sized pieces for the squirrels on the patio. Patience was beyond being simply a virtue. It was a necessity. In spite of presenting a formidable front, Milly had a softer side as well and usually, but not always, simply wanted a hug.

Visiting in someone's home, especially over an extended period of time, fosters a climate of mutual trust and generates a personal relationship that extends beyond that normally experienced in nurse-patient encounters. Lives are exposed and lifestyles revealed. Judgment on any level is inappropriate. Respect for the integrity of an individual was stressed in nursing school and has since guided my own practice. Unequivocal acceptance of a patient and family is necessary in order for a nurse or other worker to be effective. More than once I was put off by Milly's obnoxious tendencies, but then I tried to imagine myself in her shoes. How would I like to be stuck at home, hooked to an oxygen concentrator, hobbling from one room to the next, too weak to lift a milk carton? What would I be like if I were totally dependent on outside caregivers for most of my needs and having squirrels as my only other visitors? She deserved all the kindness and hugs I could offer.

Another memorable patient was Mabel, an elderly widow of a miner and a wonderful example of a hardy soul. She had lived in Victor and endured its severe winters at nearly 10,000 feet elevation since 1927. Her physician referred her for home care after she had suffered a heart attack and had refused to go to the hospital, preferring to die at home if that was to be her fate. That was no surprise, as none of these old timers wanted to go to the hospital for anything, no matter how serious.

I set out to meet Mabel, negotiating the hills and curves of the back road from Florissant to Cripple Creek, then turning south for the six winding miles to Victor. As if time stopped during the mining days, tall wooden head frames situated over open mine shafts dotted the hills. Tailings, yellow-brown piles of rock excavated in the mining process, were a common sight and added evidence of the town's history.

As I stepped onto the porch of Mabel's small frame house and raised my hand to knock, the door was opened by an elderly lady with snow white hair. She greeted me with an abrupt, "You're not here to try to make me go to the hospital, are you?" It was more like a chastising statement than a question. Respectful of Mabel's authoritative stance, I proceeded to introduce myself and was tentatively allowed entry. I quickly explained to Mabel that her doctor was agreeable to her recuperating at home as long as she would take it easy and let a nurse stop by and check on her. She accepted the plan but made me promise I wouldn't tell the doctor that she had walked to the post office and chopped wood that morning! Mabel recovered uneventfully, and her heart was undoubtedly more rested at home than it would have been in an anxiety-producing hospital environment.

Another of Prospect's nurses visited three times a week initially. She monitored Mabel's condition and medication regimen, and also volunteered to drive her to doctor appointments every two weeks for the first six weeks. Mabel received home-delivered meals and her friends came for coffee, performed the necessary household chores, and ran errands. Then Mabel began a walking program accompanied by her nurse – five minutes twice a day at first, progressing to ten and then fifteen minute walks over the ensuing weeks, finally working up to two miles. Care at home was nothing unusual for these old timers, many of whom had grown up on isolated ranches and farms, as did Mabel, and knew nothing but home treatment for illnesses and injuries. She was one of many successful home-managed patients.

Bertie, a Woodland Park widow who lived alone, was another. One benefit of small town life is that residents are attuned to the daily activities of each other and are quick to respond to a perceived need. In this case, a local pharmacist who had known Bertie for many years became concerned when he discovered her sitting on a bench in town for what seemed like an unusually long time. This spry eighty year old, who did not drive an automobile, normally walked to and from town and conducted her business on foot. When the pharmacist spoke to her, he found that she was short of breath and unable to walk home. He put Bertie in his car and drove straight to her doctor's office. An examination and blood work revealed severe congestive heart failure. Ingestion of high doses of ibuprofen for her arthritis had resulted in a gastrointestinal bleed that produced an anemia severe enough to cause the heart failure. After receiving a few units of blood in a Colorado Springs hospital, she was discharged to be followed by home care for monitoring of her fragile cardiac status. As the months went by, Bertie gained strength and her heart failure was resolved, but she didn't recover her stamina for walking to town for almost a year. She had weathered a close call, and fortunately the observant pharmacist stepped in and acted in her behalf.

Though self sufficiency was a prized attribute among mountain folks, illness at times interfered as an unwelcome intruder and compromised one's capabilities. Gertrude was a strong, independent woman in her late 60's who had lived on her own and pursued an active lifestyle for many years following the death of her husband. In the late stages of chronic pulmonary disease, she was imprisoned in her home, leashed to an oxygen concentrator. Our conversations covered life, death, and her wishes, both of us assuming she would eventually succumb to lung disease.

One day I went to her house but found no one at home. A neighbor said that Gertrude had been taken to the hospital by ambulance two days before. I was able to visit her at the hospital in Colorado Springs after begging my way into the intensive care unit. Gertrude was lying in bed, tubes everywhere, breathing with the benefit of a respirator and unable to talk. She had a terrified look on her face, totally foreign to this woman who, even in the throes of lung disease, exuded self-determination as to her care and other aspects of her life. I learned from her nurse that she had been admitted with severe abdominal pain, and tests revealed an intestinal blockage – probably colon cancer. Given the severity of her lung disease, she was a poor operative risk. There she was – hooked to every imaginable machine, helpless, and unable to communicate her end-of-life wishes. I was as horrified as she, and said something like, "Oh, my gosh, Gertrude. You certainly didn't want to end up like this, did you?" To which she shook her head to indicate a definite "no."

I went to the nurses' station and told Gertrude's nurse that we had discussed her wishes previously and that I knew she would not choose the interventions that were being administered. I also knew that not being a relative, I could do little to help with her predicament. She had no children, but fortunately, a niece and husband had been located and were on their way to the hospital. When they arrived we talked about Gertrude's wishes. They agreed that this was not the end that their aunt would have chosen.

We had the doctor paged. When he arrived, all four of us stood around Gertrude's bed and asked her if she wanted to be detached from the equipment that was prolonging her life. Her nodded "yes" was undeniable and the doctor granted her wish. Gertrude died that night, having escaped an unfortunate situation. I was thankful for our conversations about death. Most people who are experiencing serious illnesses want their wishes to be known and respected. Fortunately, advance directives are more prevalent now than in the past.

The elderly people I met provided the ongoing motivation necessary for me to endure the vicissitudes of agency administration. I loved their stories and I loved them. Hearing their tales was like taking a giant leap into the past, especially if they had lived in the area for many years and even more so if they had known my Uncle Silas and Laura Witcher. An elderly shopkeeper in Cripple Creek had not only known them but mentioned that her husband had been a pall bearer at Silas's funeral. I dug through the photos and papers my parents had sent and sure enough, there was her husband's name on the funeral program. She was excited to see this little piece of her past and to tell me some of her memories of Uncle Silas.

I met a lady who owns an antique shop in Cripple Creek and has been there for years. She was telling me what a lady's man Uncle Silas was – very good looking and smart and always had a bunch of girlfriends. She also told how much he and the boys on the ranch used to complain because Laura Witcher always made them take her along to the Saturday night dances at the Four Mile Grange Hall.

Some of the elderly folks I met had come to Colorado as pioneers. One frail antique of a lady had, as a young child, traveled west with her family in a covered wagon. Carefully preserved in a cabinet behind glass doors was the rag doll that had accompanied her on the long cross-country trip. Both showed a century of wear – the little doll, ragged and dirty, resting on a shelf, and the lady, seemingly more fragile than the doll, maneuvering unsteadily through her house from one piece of furniture to the next. Her story was fascinating. I met her when I had car trouble on the highway and hiked up the hill to her house, hoping I'd find a telephone. I found so much more.

CHAPTER 27

Prospect's Growth

The program continued to grow over the next few years. Prospect had a full contingent of staff and volunteers throughout the service area, including nurses who were more comfortable than I with highly technical hospital procedures. Because of their knowledge and skills, we were doing intravenous chemotherapy in cancer patients' homes as well as continuous morphine infusions for management of severe pain. Therapists helped rehabilitate stroke patients and others who benefited from exercise regimens to improve strength, balance, and functioning – all to enable people to live at home.

A nurse who had been carefully and attentively managing a hospice patient's infusion of pain medication through an intraspinal catheter was going to be away for the weekend, and I was going to cover for her. I wanted to meet the patient and her family and learn the details of her care, so the other nurse and I made a visit together.

There was no phone in the home, so the nurse was not aware that the patient's condition had deteriorated since her visit the previous day. When we arrived at this small cabin, the patient's daughter opened the door and announced that the patient had just died. Family members and their pastor, who had happened to stop by for a visit, were in the main room. The other nurse and I went to the bedroom to remove the morphine catheter and care for the deceased lady so that she and her surroundings would be as presentable as possible for the family.

The lifeless patient was in a small bed that was wedged into the corner of a very crowded room. We knew that the bathing and dressing process, as well as changing bed linens and straightening the room, would be difficult at best. To complicate the situation, this was a heavy woman. The other nurse and I looked at each other and rolled our eyes, communicating something like, "How in the heck are we going to do this?" Moving the bed out of the corner would have helped, but lack of space negated that solution. The wall between the bedroom and the main room was thin, so we tried to keep our conversation subdued as we contemplated various approaches that would not ruin our backs. For a few moments we were at a loss as to whether we could provide post mortem care, but we decided on an unusual approach. At least there were two of us, as neither of us could have moved this patient alone.

With inadequate space to gain any leverage, the other nurse proceeded to stand on the bed, straddling the patient and bending over from the hips, butt in the air, trying to achieve an effective stance for moving this dead weight. I provided what help I could by climbing onto the free side of the bed to try to roll the patient onto her side. While we were in these ungainly positions, struggling to turn the patient to bathe her, the unthinkable happened. We looked at each other and started laughing. A tense, problematic situation, when laughter was totally inappropriate, fueled our hysteria. No doubt it was worsened by the simple fact that there were two of us. To laugh at a time like this was horrible, but especially with family within earshot. We finally controlled ourselves and accomplished the task. I confess to this event only to show the function of humor in alleviating tension in difficult situations. Fortunately, morbid humor was normally confined to staff meetings.

* * *

In addition to the usual administrative responsibilities, meetings in Denver and other parts of the state were inordinately time consuming, especially considering the travel involved. Colorado Hospice Organization, comprised of hospice directors throughout the state, met monthly, usually in Denver, but sometimes elsewhere. Changes in home care billing procedures, all too frequent, required exhausting day-long gatherings of home care billing personnel from all over Colorado, as did revisions of instructions for completing every home care director's nemesis – the annual Medicare Cost Report. That time-consuming piece of work eventually became so complicated that it evolved into a task for a specially trained accountant who would compile data provided by the agency and produce the voluminous report for Medicare review.

August 28, 1984

I took Friday through Sunday off and then had to go to Denver on Monday. I almost fainted when I got to the office this afternoon and had about fifteen phone messages. The annual Medicare survey visit is on September 5, and I'm frantically trying to catch up on a year's worth of procrastination. I could work in the office every day from now till the 5th and still not have everything ready. Then I have to go to the state hospice meeting in Greeley the 10th and 11th and another meeting in Denver on the 14th. We are putting on a workshop the weekend of the 21st through the 23rd, and the Medicare Cost Report has to be in by the 30th.

Somewhere in there is the regular stuff – the bills and the patients. Oh, yes, and I have to write a request for an extension of the grant – new budget, etc. This is totally ridiculous and I'm going nuts. I spent two days with a newspaper reporter who produced a big story, so now I have a lot of people saying how wonderful Prospect is, and I feel like I have to keep plugging away.

Seems like I'm never home.

Trying to take care of everything – husband, kids, staff, patients, agency – was exhausting me. But I kept at it. As always, whenever I felt overwhelmed, my waning energy was bolstered by a much needed gesture of encouragement.

September 29, 1984, 12:30 a.m.

Terrible hour to be starting a letter, but I know I haven't written in ages, and there's never enough time at a reasonable hour. I've been writing thank you notes for hospice donations, and I'm tired. So much has been happening. We made it through all of the auditor's and surveyor's inspection visits with only a couple of minor problems. The grant manager and auditor were totally impressed. I finished the Medicare Cost Report after several nights of four hours of sleep this week. It is a real monster. Glad it's out of the way. Now to get to the billing (June, July, August). There's no end to the paperwork.

I totally hit the pits over the whole thing a couple of weeks ago – left home in the morning ready to give up. Then I got to my exercise group, and they told me they had decided to put on a chili supper for Prospect to thank me for leading the exercise class. What a wonderful thing for them to do. When I got out to the car, a neighbor had put a pie on the front seat so I had something to take to Help U Club. I hadn't had time to make anything to take.

Then I went to the post office to get the mail, and someone had sent a $25 check. I made a home visit, and that family gave me a $50 donation plus the use of their electric typewriter in our office for as long as we need it. Then I went to Help U Club, and they voted to give us a $100 donation. What a day that turned out to be! The chili supper was last night and was a huge success. I couldn't believe all the people – well over 100 – probably closer to 150. Lots of people put extra money in the jar, and we ended up with $515! We had our first snow yesterday – a small one -- and it was messy last night, but still lots of people came. It was great.

On Thanksgiving Day of 1984, with dinner on the table and guests at our home, I received an unusual call from the telephone repair man who had installed my private line in the house behind the country store. He was a volunteer fireman and EMT, and he needed help in an emergency situation that had become unmanageable. A toddler had drowned, reaching for a toy in a five-gallon pail of water being used to flush a non-functioning toilet. The first 911 call was for the baby, who could not be resuscitated. A second 911 call came in later to provide assistance to the frantic and distraught mother. She was agitated to the point of manifesting physical symptoms, and apparently the EMTs were considering transporting her to the hospital to be subdued with medication.

Budd and I left our guests and drove to the home in the Florissant area. Never having been in a situation anything like this, I didn't know what to expect or even how I might be able to help. I said a quick prayer asking for compassion and guidance in this profoundly sad experience.

An ambulance and a fire engine were at the house when we arrived. Firemen were standing outside on the porch near the front door. I felt overwhelmed and totally inadequate as I walked through this gauntlet of firemen into the house. The devastated mother and father were sitting together, bent over and sobbing. As I knelt on the floor in front of these grief-stricken parents and held their hands, we talked quietly. Whatever words came out of my mouth must have helped, as the situation became calm. After some unknown amount of time elapsed, I looked up and noticed that most of the firemen had left. When I felt certain that the parents were able to function and care for their other two children, I left with a promise to return the next morning.

A few weeks later the firemen invited me to give a presentation on dealing with traumatic deaths. I visited this grieving family numerous times in the ensuing months as they dealt with child protective service workers, temporary removal of the other children from the home, and subsequent marital difficulties. I was learning that home care was but one piece of a big pie, and that being part of the health care community meant helping in more ways than I ever imagined.

* * *

Keeping warm in the early months of 1985 challenged even the hardiest folks. Record lows during a two-week cold spell in February dropped the temperature to minus 40 degrees in Lake George. During that period the mercury rarely rose to zero in the daytime. Our vehicles were equipped with engine block heaters, plugged in to the house electricity, to ensure startups in the mornings. My long johns saw more than average use. Amazingly, at that altitude, a sunny day at zero, barring wind, felt warm enough to shed coat, hat, and gloves. With the addition to our house completed, we bought a second-hand hot tub with our income tax refund. What a wonderful luxury after coming in from the cold!

March 31, 1985
This snow has been wonderful. It forced me to take three days off, which I needed after two solid weeks getting ready for our state hospice licensure and Medicare hospice certification surveys. That was Wednesday and Thursday of last week and I think we did well. We have 21 patients now – more than ever before. Just admitted our 70th. Anyway, three feet of snow calls a halt to a lot of things. We didn't get to take the girls skiing. Tomorrow will be back to the

old grind for all of us. I'm so tired of working so hard. This week I'm going to try to get all the loose ends regarding the grant tied up. Then maybe get some more billing done on Saturday. I can only do it on weekends when no one is bugging me and the phone isn't ringing. One of these days I'm going to get caught up and I'm never going to get behind again. Famous last words.

CHAPTER 28

MOVING ON

In May, 1985, Leigh Anne graduated from Woodland Park High School. She spent the summer in Virginia with her father and worked there before entering Colorado State University in the fall. Budd's son Jeff, who lived with his mother elsewhere in the state, came to spend the summer with us and work for the U. S. Forest Service doing trail maintenance. Joyce's daughter Michelle continued to live with us, though her adjustment to our blended family had not been smooth.

At 9,000 feet altitude, our climate had two seasons: winter and July. Summer, short as it was, provided time for cutting and stacking the next winter's supply of firewood and squeezing in a few weekend camping trips.

August 2, 1985
Hospice is fine. We have $30,000 in our savings account, and I think that will see us through another year. We had $8,000 in donations last year. We made 1,772 patient visits,

over twice as many as the year before. We took care of 52 people. We got our hospice state licensure and Medicare certification in June for another year, and we have our home health agency Medicare certification survey visit next week. I'm not as far behind as usual, so I'm not going nuts at the moment. Next weekend we sell drinks at a local event. It's a lot of work for a little money, but it helps Prospect become more visible.

As much as I complained about the overwhelming amount of paperwork, I usually managed to keep my head above water. September was always a difficult month for me, with the Medicare Cost Report due on the 30th.

September 11, 1985
I have to go out on the Elkhorn Road to see a patient who just came home from the hospital and has to have a dressing change today. His nurse is out of town. I'll never get to the cost report. How frustrating. Fall is definitely here – Cold nights with hard freezes. No more summer clothes around here.

Prospect's growth continued, though the patient census fluctuated and gave rise to anxious and sometimes discouraging days. Fortunately, by 1986, there were enough nurses on staff for Budd and me to take a few days off to ski or simply escape. Those little excursions put me behind on office work, but I needed the time away.

* * *

Our lives took an unexpected turn in the spring of 1986 when Budd injured his back. Physical therapy helped initially and enabled us to take an all-expense-paid trip that we had won – a week in Hawaii – in June. We spent the first few days enjoying Oahu's north shore and then flew to the island of Kauai for the remainder of the week. Budd's back felt so much better in that climate that he entertained thoughts of possibly living there.

We had noticed a sign at a condominium complex for unbelievably under-priced units. We met with the real estate agent and learned that they were the remaining unsold condominiums in a retirement complex. We signed a contract on a one-bedroom unit, having no idea at the time how we would pay for it. The minimum age to live in the complex was 45, and we did not yet meet the requirement, but the real estate agent told us that she knew of a lady who would want to rent our unit. She also knew of a person on the island who would lend us the money for a down payment. So off we went to meet this lady who had money to spare. We must have seemed trustworthy enough, because we left her place with a $10,000 check in hand. Amazing how things work out.

The time in Hawaii gave me a chance to relax and think about our future, given that Budd would probably not be able to continue doing the demanding physical work that had been his livelihood. I realized how exhausted I had become and that my tank was often running on empty. Maybe it was time for us to consider making a change. Kauai was indeed a tropical paradise – a kind of beauty that was vastly different from our mountains.

We returned home considering new possibilities. I was pleased to see that Prospect survived without me. We mortgaged our house to pay for the condominium. Having a renter in it not only covered the loan payments, it also gave us time to consider the feasibility of such an extreme relocation. While a move was not an immediate possibility, the idea gave us a new focus and something other than back trouble to occupy our minds and conversations.

As summer progressed, Budd's back worsened. He was frustrated at the implications of limited function – not being able to earn a living, cut our firewood, and perform other chores necessary for living in the mountains. In a final attempt to avoid back surgery, he entered an inpatient pain management program in a Colorado Springs hospital. When the referring physician recommended that he go there, she said it was as much for me as for him – that I looked like I needed a good night's sleep. I was indeed stretched beyond my limits, dealing with Budd's injury, managing Prospect, and caring for Budd's son, who had come to live with us for his senior year of high school. By then step-daughter Michelle had gone to Ohio to live with her father, and Leigh Anne was back at Colorado State, so at least there was only one child at home.

The Pain Clinic program, similar to a watered-down version of boot camp, did help Budd. He continued to do the prescribed exercise program at home, but throughout the fall, he realized that our cold, changeable weather, with frequent barometric pressure variations, was aggravating his back problem. He was better than the weatherman at forecasting our storms.

Budd wanted to go back to Kauai. I found inexpensive airline tickets and a place to stay on the beach for $22 per night and made reservations. Looking forward to two weeks on Kauai in January and February provided much-needed diversion from the discouragement we both felt.

In an attempt to take some of the pressure off myself and to prepare for my two-week absence, I hired some helpers. This was long overdue, but had been dependent on finding capable office staff as well as the means to pay them.

October 28, 1986

Yesterday was pretty good because one of the nurses and I spent all afternoon dividing up the administrative and secretarial duties between her, me, and one of our home health aides who has been volunteering in the office. She is now going to be paid for eight hours a week to do the billing starting December 1. There is a new nurse who is interested in learning the administrative side of the job and is (I hope) going to start working for 8 to 12 hours per week. I haven't talked to her yet, and she might not be interested for only $6 per hour. My idea is to get her started before I leave on vacation. I don't know how I think I'm going to teach her plus get caught up, but it's worth a try.

I didn't get as much done today as I had planned because I got called out to a patient as soon as I got to the office this morning and didn't get back till 11:00 a.m. Then a family member of another patient came in and talked for an hour this afternoon. The man who owns our building and has the computerized accounting service that we are getting for $75 per month spent about 1½ hours with me going over our accounting needs. Somewhere in there I managed to do a Medicare appeal on a denied claim and the first form for our corporate tax return. I keep hoping I can get to the billing. Maybe next week.

I'll bet you get so sick of hearing nothing but how far behind I always am. Actually, I've been fairly well caught up about twice in the past year, but it never seems to last. I really am starting to think about winding down my hospice experience. My goal for the next six months is to have other people functioning well enough to run the place without me.

January 12, 1987
The new grant came in. Prospect is $9,876 richer. Not bad for about four hours of work! I'm spending most of it on office help and some on equipment and educational materials. We just had a big secretarial desk, electric typewriter, three-drawer file cabinet, and a bookcase donated from the home of a patient who died. Our room looks like a real office now instead of a disaster area. Each person has a work area instead of everyone sharing one table. We are looking for a cheap storage unit so we can get the walkers, bedside commodes and tub benches out of here.

The nurse who has the administrative interests isn't working out, but the wife of one of our volunteers is looking like she could run the office by herself. She is well organized, and can do a lot of what I do. She's coming in a day and a half each week now.

January 27, 1987
I did really well getting ready to go on vacation. I did have to work all day Saturday and then again yesterday morning before we left, but I got everything done. I have a wonderful office person 16 hours per week now, and she can do just about everything in the office. This is the first time in almost five years that I've been able to leave for two weeks.

Having the billing and other office work taken care of was a great relief. One of the nurses was capable of supervising the patient care aspect, so with all angles covered, I felt comfortable leaving.

Once again, Kauai's warm, humid weather relieved Budd's back and leg pain. We could see that he needed a different climate in order to heal. While we were at the retirement complex checking on our rental condominium, the real estate agent showed us a two-bedroom unit, never lived in, that had fallen out of escrow. It must have been intended for us. On our way to the airport, we had stopped at the Florissant post office to pick up our mail. In it was a check from the sale of my Virginia house, which had been purchased by its renters. We signed a contract on the larger condominium and decided to make the move. I would turn 45 in July and we would qualify for residency.

We were ready for a change. Leigh Anne was happily ensconced at Colorado State University; Jeff would graduate from Woodland Park High School in June and move to California with friends; and Michelle continued to live with her father in Ohio. We were free to go!

The time had come for me to let go of Prospect. It was like seeing a child grow up and leave home to become a success of his or her own making. I knew I would miss Prospect's wonderful staff and my last patient – Milly, whom I had known for five years. As a parting gift, she insisted that I take a plate that her mother had brought with her when she emigrated from England. Along with the inevitable sadness in leaving was knowing that I could enjoy the rewards of hard work and the satisfaction that comes from having done something worthwhile. Capable staff could and would carry on. While I never expected the Prospect experience to be an easy ride, at times it proved to require more time and effort than I had envisioned. Ignorance may not be bliss, but it surely does keep us from avoiding challenges that can enrich our lives.

CHAPTER 29

FINAL THOUGHTS

Trading a secure career in the East for a jobless move to Colorado probably was about as irrational as taking a fur coat to Hawaii. In my wildest dreams I never could have fathomed the adventure that lay ahead. And that is probably a good thing, or I might not have done it.

When I went to nursing school in the early 1960's, nurses were beginning to be acknowledged as independent thinkers, but continued to be relegated to roles as doctors' assistants. The high-tech equipment available to nurses in hospitals today was unknown in 1960. Students were taught meticulous observational skills and to be intuitive in problem solving. These abilities served me well. If I had to carry out a nursing procedure with which I was unfamiliar, I drove to a Colorado Springs hospital before a patient was discharged and learned what was to be done. Gaining such knowledge gave me confidence in my previously underdeveloped hands-on nursing skills.

My pre-Colorado life laid the groundwork for this endeavor in the mountains. No matter how boring a task, how tedious an academic exercise, or how unexciting life was at a particular time, I learned something at every juncture – something with a payoff down the road. Years of public health nursing practice and administration, nursing and graduate education, and a wealth of life experiences laid a foundation for directing a home care and hospice agency and serving its patients and families. Though the Denver Hospice prepared me well, every situation was new and different, and I always expected the unexpected. I tried to exhibit confidence, even when I might not have felt it. Families and patients needed to sense that, and I knew I would be able to guide them through their experience, even as I learned something new along with them.

Agency administration was difficult and became inordinately time consuming, especially as the program grew. The more problematic it became, the more I embraced the challenge to do it successfully. In the words of my father, "You can do anything if you put your mind to it." I must have believed him.

My discomfort with life in the D.C. suburbs had puzzled me for years. The journey to the mountains, replete with life-changing events, challenges, and people, connected me to my past and gave me a home that truly felt like home.

Offering a service that provided care, guidance and support needed by people in the community was an opportunity for me to give to others. I am convinced that sharing something of ourselves with people in our lives becomes a mission statement for each of us. In my case, the tally was lopsided. I received so much more than I gave.

Among the many gifts I received, none was greater than being allowed into the lives of patients and families at a very sensitive and fragile time. People living out their final weeks and days have so much to teach the rest of us, as we plod through the tedium of our daily lives, wondering in what direction we are headed and how we will get through the coming months and years.

First and foremost they teach us that dying is in many instances okay. Or even welcome. Notwithstanding sudden, unexpected death, for all of us there will come a time when a diseased or worn out body needs to be cast off. It is as much a part of life as is birth.

We learn the importance of doing things on our "bucket list" and nurturing important relationships. We see that life can be far shorter than we thought it would be and that our priorities need unfailing attention.

We learn that healing comes in many forms. And not necessarily what we had in mind.

We marvel at the power of one's will to live or die and even to choose a time to die.

Most importantly, we learn not to give up hope, even if it is simply hope for a better day.

And we never forget that miracles *do* happen.

Mountain living taught me the importance of interdependence with other people, resourcefulness, and the satisfaction of living a simple life. It showed me how much I could do without. I learned to appreciate a life rich in experiences and meaningful relationships rather than possessions. For mountain dwellers, treasured independence and self-sufficiency are strengthened through their relationships with other mountain people. While privacy is valued and respected, there is a certain comfort in knowing that the neighbor down the road will dig you out of the snow or figure out why your chain saw won't start. A need for help draws rural people together. Strong emotional bonds reinforce basic values sometimes absent in urban lifestyles. Materialism and "keeping up with the Joneses" are foreign concepts. What one wears or lives in or drives has nothing to do with status among these down-to-earth folks. They dress for comfort. They drive what will get them where they need to go, carrying or towing what they need to transport. Strength of character, ability to "tough it out," willingness to give to others, reverence for nature, and an appreciation of a mountain lifestyle are key to getting along. Lacking these attributes, one does not last long in the mountains.

My Christian beliefs sustained me through all of my adventures and experiences. I prayed a lot and always felt God's guidance through uncertainties. God and I had many conversations regarding my safety, especially out at night in snowstorms, and Prospect's survival against sometimes seemingly insurmountable odds. I prayed for guidance in every home death, that I would have the right words to help each family and that the event would be peaceful. The angel God had placed on my shoulder came through for me time after time. The helpers who were there for me were my earthly angels. They always appeared on cue.

Interacting with people nearing the end of life and witnessing bodies in a state of decline inspired me to be thankful for every healthy day that enabled me to do the work I loved in a beautiful place. How many people have the good fortune to live out their passion? Most importantly, I learned that true joy comes from walking with others through the bumps and detours of their lives and helping them move on to their next chapter. I never ceased to be amazed, as I crested Wilkerson Pass, drove across South Park, up the Tarryall Road to Jefferson, or down the back road to Cripple Creek and Victor, that I was doing a job. To me it was a wonderful adventure.

Epilogue

My west-facing living room window frames a picture-perfect view of 14,269-foot Mt. Antero and a pure white plume of snow blowing off of its majestic peak. The wind is howling through the ponderosas. Earlier today Budd, Chico, and I ventured down our creek trail on a five-mile hike. It was one of those coat-on, coat-off, crazy-weather days when fast moving clouds and bursts of snow showers interrupted the warm sun. Later, to placate our complaining knees, we indulged in a soak at the hot springs up the road. Budd is napping with a tired little dog nestled beside him. It has been a perfect day in the Colorado Rockies.

The old 76 Ranch is about an hour or so from where I live now, and I visit there from time to time. I've been in Uncle Silas's office and in the upstairs bedroom where Mom and Dad stayed. The area immediately surrounding the ranch house has been subdivided into a few parcels occupied by tasteful western homes, but it is still "my" place.

Prospect's original service area is not as desolate as it was in the early 1980's. Many more homes dot the landscape, and paved roads are more prevalent. Most places now have electricity and telephone service.

Prospect Home Care and Hospice has continued to grow. It is now located in a spacious office complex in the hospital in Woodland Park. Thirty staff and 250 volunteers provide care to patients and families and support for the agency. Prospect now offers services that I could never have imagined in a much expanded, multi-faceted program serving the area.

Kauai was a healing place for us. Budd became resident manager of our condominium complex. I served on the Board of Kauai Hospice and ended a 30-year nursing career directing Kauai's public health nursing program. After six wonderful years of island living we returned to the mainland and devoted a few years to exploring the country in a small motor home. For several years we lived in southern New Mexico in an old adobe home that we restored. Then finally, after 20 years of running from cold weather, we returned to Colorado, where Budd and I know that we belong. I am at home here and will be forever thankful that when the mountains called so many years ago, I listened and I came.

Made in United States
Orlando, FL
23 October 2022